ASPECTS OF BLACKBURN

ASPECTS *of* BLACKBURN

Discovering Local History

Edited by
Alan Duckworth

Series Editor
Brian Elliott

Wharncliffe Publishing Limited

**First Published in 1999 by
Wharncliffe Publishing Limited
an imprint of
Pen and Sword Books Limited,
47 Church Street, Barnsley,
South Yorkshire. S70 2AS**

Copyright © Wharncliffe Publishing Limited 1999

*For up-to-date information on other titles produced under the
Wharncliffe imprint, please telephone or write to:*

> **Wharncliffe Publishing Limited
> FREEPOST
> 47 Church Street
> Barnsley
> South Yorkshire S70 2BR
> Telephone (24 hours): 01226 - 734555**

ISBN: 1-871647-56-8

A CIP catalogue record of this book is available from the
British Library

Cover illustration: Salford Bridge, Blackburn. *Courtesy of Blackburn Libraries.*

Printed in Great Britain by
Redwood Books, Trowbridge, Wiltshire

CONTENTS

INTRODUCTION

by Alan Duckworth

What's a Yorkshireman doing editing a book on Blackburn? Well back in the 1920s my grandfather, who was a millwright came to Blackburn to work on a mill engine. He had a bull nosed Morris and brought my father with him for the ride. When he'd finished the job, the manager treated them both to pie and peas on the market. My father was in the dickey seat of the car going back. He threw his cap out and after a mile or two informed my grandfather who had to turn back. My father got a clip round the ear for his trouble, but it was worth it to prolong the adventure.

Thirty years later I came to Blackburn to take up a post in the town's Reference Library. I've lived in the area ever since. Over the years I've met many people with great knowledge and enthusiasm for the history of the town and have been lucky enough to be able to recruit some of them as contributors to this book.

Nobody knows the Leeds-Liverpool Canal better than Mike Clarke and his piece on the boatyard at Whitebirk is so vivid and informative you can almost smell the sawdust. Hubert Hartley's family have been in cotton for over two hundred years and the story of his family is the story of the industry itself.

Three pieces view nineteenth century Blackburn from different points of view, providing a multi-dimensional picture of the town. Jim Heyes uses the diaries of Charles Tiplady to build up a picture of the man. Tiplady was a Tory and a pillar of the establishment, quite unlike Bill Turner's subject, William Beesley, a Chartist and passionate advocate of the rights of common people. The political context of the time is described by Matthew Cole.

Tiplady was a pioneer librarian and witnessed the laying of the foundation stone of Blackburn's new public library. Bob Snape describes what kind of reading material was on offer to the public in those early days. Stephen Child gives us an account of Catholicism in Blackburn and Ashok Chudasama provides an insight into what it was like for those immigrants arriving in the town in the 1960s.

Politicians of all parties are fond of having local government boundaries drawn and redrawn; thus Lancastrians end up in Yorkshire and Yorkshire folk become Lancastrians. Twenty five years ago Blackburn and Darwen were yoked together. It's not an arrangement that the citizens of either town would have voted for, but it does give me the opportunity of including some interesting contributions in the book, which properly speaking should be entitled *Aspects of Blackburn with Darwen*, echoing the Borough's new designation.

Jan Gill and Mary Whittaker take us on a tour of Darwen's blue plaques, an encouragement to anybody who fancies combining a walk with a look at the town's history. Graham Groom tells the tale of the Darwen Spitfire and I recount the story of that most famous of Darwen's monuments: the Jubilee Tower.

Gillian Hall and Susan O'Malley give a fascinating account of Calderstones Hospital in Whalley. Oddly enough the bureaucrats failed to include Whalley in Blackburn, but for most of the people who live there Blackburn is their natural centre. Many work or have worked in Blackburn and of all the many hundreds who have been on the staff at Calderstones over the years, the vast majority have travelled there from their homes in Blackburn.

I tell the story of Darwen's famous artist James Morton, and Joe Wharton gives us the history of Corporation Park. Finally, I round everything off with Worker's Playtime, a look at the growth of leisure after the Industrial Revolution.

It has been a privilege and a pleasure to put this book together. Myself and all the contributors hope it will be read with enjoyment and that it will add another chapter to the history of this part of Lancashire. It doesn't stop here however. The publishers are keen for this to be but the first in a whole series of volumes, so if any of you out there feel you have a story to tell, please get in touch with me c/o Wharncliffe Books, 47 Church Street, Barnsley S70 2AS.

I would like to thank the staff at Blackburn and Darwen libraries for all their help, also the staff at Wharncliffe for all their hard work, encouragement and advice.

The *Aspects Series* has already covered the Yorkshire towns of Barnsley, Rotherham, Doncaster, Sheffield, Wakefield, Leeds, Huddersfield, Bradford, Hull and the Yorkshire Coast. Now Blackburn, Accrington and Birmingham have been added. Nationwide coverage is imminent.

Anyone interested in making a contribution to *Aspects of Blackburn 2* should in the first instance, contact Mr Alan Duckworth Editor, c/o Wharncliffe Books, 47 Church Street, Barnsley S70 2AS, enclosing a brief description of the proposed work.

1. From Ghosties and Ghoulies and Long-Leggety Beasties and Things That Go Bump in the Night Good Lord, Deliver Us!

by Alan Duckworth

THINGS REALLY WERE GOING BUMP IN THE NIGHT in a house at High Lumb Hole in Darwen a hundred years ago. It was on the Green (Figure 1), which, despite its name, was a mean part of town, a warren of cheap lodgings and malodorous dwellings. Even in this company the house had an evil reputation. It was said to be haunted and nobody would live there at any price. In desperation, the landlord offered it at no price, in other words, rent free, and a couple, plus their son, couldn't resist the offer.

The first few nights were peaceful, as though whatever haunted it was savouring the moment, or lulling its victims into a false sense of security. Then one night the family was awakened by a din as though all their sticks of furniture were cavorting madly round the house downstairs. They lay in their beds, frozen with horror, then came a

Figure 1. The Green, an area with a sinister reputation. *Darwen Library*

crashing sound as though their precious bits of crockery were being smashed on the floor. They ran down to investigate. All was as still as the grave; nothing had been disturbed; all was as it had been when they had gone upstairs to bed.

This was repeated night after night with varying degrees of ferocity. Once it sounded as if every window in the house had been shattered, but, on investigation, it was found that they were all intact. It says something about the stoicism of our ancestors, or perhaps what they would put up with to save a few bob on the rent, that the family stuck this out for two years before their nerves finally failed them and they left. The house remained empty. Nobody ever attempted to live there again. When the area was at last being cleared, and all the houses were being pulled down, much interest was centred on the haunted one. When workmen lifted its stone floor they found a further layer of stone flags, and, beneath these, an abomination of tangled bones which stank dreadfully!

No doubt long-leggety beasties have been stalking the imagination of dwellers on the West Pennine Moors for thousands of years, possibly ever since the stone circle was constructed at Turton Heights, or the Bronze age burials were taking place at Ashleigh Barrow. Interestingly, people were still afraid of passing Ashleigh Barrow at night, even after its purpose had long been forgotten. It wasn't until 1864, when the foundations of Ashleigh House were being dug that the charred remains of a number of bodies came to light, packed into urns, which are now on display at Darwen Library.

There is a more modern settlement of the dead up the hill from Ashleigh at Whitehall; the municipal cemetery opened in 1861, it's a sinister place at night, with headstones and monuments canted at awkward angles, and graves sunken and twisted, as though the dead are not at rest. They say a figure in white can sometimes be seen flitting fretfully about the graves.

The Romans came this way too, along a road they constructed to the east of Darwen, the Roman Road. No doubt they brought with them their own fears and superstitions, culled from the pagan pantheons of the Mediterranean, of from the darker deities of the fringes of the Empire. Did they leave something of this behind them? The owner of a farm on the Roman Road at Blacksnape thinks they did. He has encountered a number of strange happenings: the sudden appearance of blood in the bath; a strong aroma of tobacco in a house where nobody smokes; doors that are tugged shut from within when you try to open them; the piano that plays when there's nobody in the room; the mischievous pushes in the back when people are going down the stairs. The ghost's predilection for tobacco and piano music argue against a Roman origin, but nothing in the history of the building offers an explanation, and a glance at the Ordnance Survey map suggests there was nothing on the site before the farm was built.

Another fold in the hills, and another strange tale. From Pickup Bank near Hoddlesden comes the legend of the dragon, four or five yards long with great, glaring eyes and talons like an eagle. It terrorised the local population for years, until they found they could control its depredations by offering a daily sacrifice of sheep. This worked well until one winter a great blizzard came that lasted three days and three nights. Many sheep perished on the bleak hill. The dragon began to prey on other livestock and domestic pets, even children were at risk. The people turned to the local squire, named Grimshaw, for help. He confronted the beast in its den and with a few well aimed arrows put an end to its reign of terror once and for all.

There's something elemental about the moorland hills, something that Emily Brontë must have recognised when she described Cathy's ghost ranging among them seeking Heathcliff. They are like the sea; vast, dark, seemingly featureless, but with hidden depths where lurk brooding mysteries. Perhaps this is how they seemed once to a certain rambler on his way back to his car, parked at the car-park near the Royal Arms in Tockholes, after a day spent walking over Darwen Moors. He'd left it a little late for his return; the Irish Sea was already a red line ruled by the sun along the western horizon, and in the east over Pendle, the first stars were out. He took the path which curves round to the north of the Tower, too late now to climb up it for the view, and began to descend towards Step Back. Perhaps it was the glimpse of Pendle which had put the image of a frightening old woman into his mind. Perhaps long ago he'd heard the story of the ghost at Step Back and relegated it to his subconscious, from where it was now stirring, but as he approached a jumble of stones that had once been a dwelling, he saw something move among them.

Night was gaining fast and the light was uncertain, but surely there was a figure there, an old woman in a black shawl. Instinct prompted him to turn from the path and flee headlong down the moor, but his reason stayed him. It could all be a trick of the shadows, or a woman, a real woman, in distress, or in need of help.

In distress she was, but long beyond any earthly power to help. She turned her white face towards him and held up white hands in supplication, but it was the whiteness of bone, not of flesh.

For a few moments he had no control of his limbs, then he did, and

Figure 2. 'Old Aggie's', when it was a haven for thirsty walkers. *Author*

he fled, running as though the Devil himself were after him. He didn't stop until he was back at his car and even then, as he fumbled with his key in the lock, he dreaded to see one of those fearfully long, white hands reaching out of the darkness for him.

Later, much later, when his nerve was restored, he did a little research and discovered that the ruin at Step Back had once been a farmhouse known as 'Old Aggie's', where 'Old Aggie' herself had provided refreshment for travellers (Figure 2). It became a popular spot and word got round that she had a hoard of gold hidden away. The legend has it that she was murdered one night, that her money was stolen and that her ghost walks, vainly seeking it. Whatever the truth of the matter, Step Back might be a good place to avoid when the sun is going down over the Irish Sea.

A little over a mile away lies another ruin that you would do well to avoid after dusk: Hollinshead Hall. This was the Manor House for Tockholes, built in the eighteenth century. Photographs are rare, so the one reproduced here (Figure 3) is worth its place, despite its poor quality. Before the Hall, there had been other buildings here, records as far back as the fourteenth century refer to them.

There's not much to see now, but in a corner of the garden is a curious well-house which has the air of a place of worship, but not a

Figure 3. Hollinshead Hall in a ruinous state. *Darwen Library*

Christian one (Figure 4). A carved stone head, probably of a lion, dribbles water which gathers in stone cisterns on either side of it. There are stone benches along each wall, and channels in the floor. The building was restored in 1905 by public subscription. It is said that people caught in sudden snowstorms have had to spend the night here, and have never been the same afterwards.

The main house has its ghosts: that of a lady said to have been the wife of the Squire, murdered by him when he took a fancy to his housekeeper. A tramp was found hanging in the ruins once, and his ghost is said to walk, as is that of a boy dressed in the fashion of years gone by. Even in broad daylight with the bees buzzing and the cars beetling along the road to Bolton down below, there's an eerie, otherworldly atmosphere about the place.

Originally Turton Tower was just that, just a tower, just a crude, square fortification built perhaps as early as the twelfth century, when raids from

Figure 4. The well house at Hollinshead Hall. *Darwen Library*

Scotland were still to be feared. By the sixteenth century, much had been added to provide accommodation more suited to prosperous and peaceful times (Figure 5). Additions and modifications continued up until last century. The Tower was presented to the Urban District Council in 1930.

It's no surprise that such an ancient place has its ghosts; the lady on the stairs, whose rustling silk dress can plainly be heard, and the oak cradle dated 1630 that can be seen rocking by itself. Most celebrated of all is the mystery surrounding the two skulls that rest on the Bradshaw family bible in a display case in the Cheetham Room. These were found in Bradshaw Brook in about 1750. They were placed on the mantelpiece at Timberbottom Farm, now demolished. Almost at once the house was plagued by disturbances: the rattling of crockery; the sound of heavy footsteps on the stairs; and the ghostly re-enactment of a duel between two ghostly cavaliers, with a ghostly girl looking on.

The skulls were given a decent burial in Bradshaw churchyard, but the haunting persisted. Only when the skulls were placed on the family bible in Bradshaw Hall was peace restored. Later they were moved to Turton Tower, with no further disturbances, apart from the time one of the skulls was removed for conservation. You can be sure it was quickly replaced.

You might think the twentieth century, bringing with it the triumph of science and reason, would have seen the end of ghosts, but, however safe and cosy you feel with the electric light on and the central heating purring away, once they are turned off, and the darkness and the cold begin to reassert themselves, then the old fears return, the shadows in the corner become sinister, and we pray once again to be delivered from 'ghosties and ghoulies and long-leggety beasties.'

Figure 5. Turton Tower. *Author*

2. THE HARTLEYS: TWO HUNDRED AND SIXTY-ONE YEARS IN THE TEXTILE INDUSTRY

by Hubert Hartley

IN 1730 SIR ROBERT WALPOLE was Prime Minister, being the first to hold that office, George II was on the throne and Blackburn had a population of fewer than 4,000. In that year the Overseers of the Poor of the town placed one of their charges, Thomas Hartley, as an indentured apprentice with Robert Kenyon, a check weaver. Thomas Hartley was my great, great, great great, grandfather. It was the duty of the Overseers to relieve the sick and aged, and to apprentice any children of vagrant couples who trespassed into their parish, (even against their will) thus relieving the parish of a charge on the Poor Rate. This indenture, which is in the Lancashire Record Office, is hand written, fairly lengthy and makes interesting reading, but tells us nothing about Thomas except that he was a poor boy of Blackburn. His age is not mentioned, nor are his parents and it must be a matter for conjecture whether they had died, or had abandoned him.

All cloth was woven on handlooms at the time (Figure 1) and it was arduous work, men doing the weaving on the looms whilst the women did the spinning and other ancilliary jobs. There were probably about 1,000 looms in the area, as many of the townspeople had a loom in their home on which they produced cloth for a dealer, or, if they owned the loom, for their own use, any surplus being sold in order to supplement their meagre income. Incidentally, when reading old documents such as wills, one often finds mention of a pair of looms. This in fact refers to one loom, the term 'pair' has the same meaning as when used in 'a pair of scissors' or a 'pair of trousers'; there being only one item, which is composed of two connected parts, in the case of a loom these being the warp and the weft.

In 1733, John Kay of Bury invented the flying-shuttle which enabled production to increase. On 15 April 1740, Thomas Hartley married Margaret Barker in Blackburn Parish Church and from this union they had four daughters and one son. Thomas had evidently made good progress as a weaver as he became an apprentice master and taught the trade to several boys. His burial is recorded in the burial register of Blackburn Parish Church on 2 January 1759.

Figure 1. Handloom, reputedly the last one in use in Darwen, owned by the Eccles family of Chapels. *Darwen Library*

Thomas's son, also named Thomas, was baptised at Blackburn Parish Church on 14 March 1756. He followed his father's trade, and also became an apprentice master. He married Betty Hacking on 21 May 1780 and they had eight children; six girls and two boys.

Several of the children died in infancy; Betty died in October 1801, and Thomas the following January.

The census of 1801 was the first ever, and Blackburn's population was 11,980. There were about 7,000 handlooms in the town, most of which were owned by manufacturers. Events of great importance to the cotton industry had occurred in 1764, when James Hargreaves invented the Spinning Jenny, and again in 1769 when Richard Arkwright invented the water frame, and erected a spinning mill. King George III succeeded to the throne in 1760 and he reigned until 1820.

The youngest son of Thomas and Betty, my great, great, grandfather, was named John and was born in 1797. By the time he was five years old both his parents had died, and, as none of his siblings was an adult and able to look after him, he was taken into care by the Overseers of the Poor until he reached eight years of age. Two months before the Battle of Trafalgar in 1805, John was put out as an apprentice to Richard Aspden, to learn the trade of a weaver (until the age of twenty-one) just as had happened to his grandfather Thomas in 1730.

On 31 January 1824, John married Susannah Woods. This was a time of deep depression in the weaving trade. A few years earlier, in 1818, 6,000 handloom weavers had marched to Woodfold Park to demand a pay increase from Henry Sudell because of the extreme hardship they were enduring, but when powerlooms were introduced to the area in 1825, the situation worsened. The population of Blackburn then numbered about 23,000, and there were 7,000 handlooms and 216 powerlooms in the town. Powerlooms had been in use for several years but were not successful, until the one patented by William Horrocks in 1802 was improved by Sharp and Roberts in 1822.

John Hartley's first child, Joseph, was born in January 1826 at the height of the depression in Blackburn. Most handloom weavers had no work and, for the fortunate few who did, their wages for a sixteen hour day, were insufficient to feed a family. Whole families were starving and petitions were sent to Parliament. Many weavers were convinced that the power loom was to blame for their troubles. In April 1826 an estimated 6,000 people rioted and 212 powerlooms at the Dandy Factory and 25 looms at John Haughton's mill in Grimshaw Park were wrecked. The High Constable's men arrested several of the rioters and John Hartley was among these. The ring leaders were committed for trial at the Quarter Sessions but John never appeared there. It is probable that he had not been a serious offender and was released without a trial.

King George IV came to the throne in 1820 and after him in 1830, William IV reigned until 1837, when Queen Victoria was proclaimed sovereign. In the years between 1828 and 1842, the Poor Law Amendment Act tightened relief in Britain and the Tolpuddle Martyrs were persecuted to discourage working class organisation. In Blackburn in August 1842, because of wage reductions and the depression, workers rioted in what became known as the 'Plug Riots'. This was because they pulled out the plugs in the mill boilers and so stopped the mills running.

Six more children were born to John and Susannah between 1828 and 1839 and their last child was born in 1842. In the 1841 census of Blackburn, John is shown living in Jackson Street with his wife, four sons and two daughters. At this time there were about 3,000 handlooms and 6,000 powerlooms in Blackburn, being operated by approximately 8,000 people; the population at that time was 36,629. It was in this year that William Kenworthy and James Bullough of Blackburn, patented the weft stop motion and several other refinements which greatly improved the efficiency of the powerloom.

In the 1851 census, John, his wife, two sons and three daughters were living at 2, Little Peel where he was described as a handloom weaver. There were only 500 handlooms running; the number of powerlooms had risen to 12,000 and the population had reached 46,536. John died in the early 1860s, his wife Susannah lived a further ten years and is buried in Blackburn cemetery in what was known as the 'Common Ground', which was where most of the poor people were buried. There is no memorial stone marking the grave and it can certainly be said that John and his wife, who had been born poor and lived through times of hardship and deprivation, died as poor as they had lived.

Understandably, John had been no lover of powerlooms and when his eldest son, Joseph was old enough, there being very little opportunity for work outside the textile trade, John encouraged him to go into a spinning mill. Joseph began as an ancilliary worker, cleaning the machines and doing odd jobs. In 1841 he was a piecer, in 1851 a spinner, and later became supervisor of a section of spindles and was given a sum of money for the yarn produced out of which he paid the people who worked for him.

Joseph married Mary Lowe on 18 August 1855 and at this time there were about 20,000 powerlooms but very few handlooms operating in Blackburn. In 1861 the Civil War in America caused great hardship to the cotton workers of Lancashire as the blockade

The Knocker Up. 5.30 A.M.
How the Lancashire Mill Worker is roused
from his Slumbers.

Figure 2. The Knocker-up. *Accrington Library*

of the Confederate ports prevented raw cotton being exported. Once again there were bad times, mass unemployment and famine, and Joseph and his family suffered along with the rest.

When the war ended in 1865, Joseph went back to work as a spinner until about 1880 when, as this was a demanding job, he took work as a labourer for several years before retiring. Even then he did not stay idle, becoming a 'knocker-up' (Figure 2) and he is described as such in the 1891 census. The knocker-up began work at 5.00 am and finished about two hours later. He had to wake people up so that they would not be late for work. He had a long pole with wires on the end which he would rattle on the window of his clients' bedrooms and there are many humorous stories regarding this occupation in Lancashire folk-lore.

Joseph and Mary had five children, but only three of them lived to adulthood. Joseph died in September 1893, but Mary lived until 1911 and they are both buried in the same grave at Pleasington Priory. The number of powerlooms had risen steadily to 79,403 by 1907 but by this time there were no hand looms left in use. The population of Blackburn had reached about 120,000 and was still rising. Queen Victoria had died in 1901 when King Edward VII became the Sovereign. He reigned until 1910 when his son became King George V.

The three children of Joseph and Mary who survived went first of all into the cotton mill. One of them, Robert, (Figure 3) who was born in 1862, married Ann McHugh in 1882. Ann was a weaver, and they had probably met in the mill but, by the time, of their marriage he was employed by a local brewery. As his father's uncle was a publican, some influence might have been used by him to get Robert placed in this job. Robert's younger sister Elizabeth Alice, who was born in 1867, was a cotton winder for many years, and did not marry.

Robert and Ann had eight children, but four of them died in infancy and one died unmarried aged thirty

Figure 3. Robert Hartley, about 1900. *Author*

one. The other three also entered the cotton trade and were employed in a variety of occupations: Edward became a weaver, Joseph became a cloth inspector in the warehouse, and Mary Elizabeth, who never married, became a cotton winder.

Joseph was my father.(Figure 4). He was born in 1888 and began work in a cotton mill as a warehouse boy when he was

Figure 4. Joseph Hartley in 1916. *Author*

fourteen and made steady progress, qualifying as a warehouseman by the time he was twenty-one. By the year 1907, the number of powerlooms in Blackburn had risen to 79,405 and Lancashire's cotton goods were in demand all over the world. The Great War, now known as World War One, began in August 1914 and Joseph joined the Royal Artillery in March 1916.

He was gassed and wounded twice while serving in France and Flanders but survived and was released from the Army in 1920. He married my mother, Mary Fitton, in 1916 and they had four sons born between 1920 and 1926. In common with other cotton workers Joseph had to endure the slumps which occurred with increasing frequency, and had to travel to other parts of the country in search of work. He eventually obtained a position at a mill in Accrington. He did essential work during World War Two and returned to work for his former employers at their Blackburn mill after the War. He died in Haston Lee Mill, Blackburn, in September, 1950 where he was the warehouse manager.

The number of looms in Blackburn had reached the high point of over 94,000 by 1917 and stayed at about that figure until 1924 (Figure 5). Hard times came again to the cotton trade and in the next ten years the number of looms fell by a half. In 1937 the number was

Figure 5. Looms at Bank Top Mill, decorated for Edward V11's coronation. *Darwen Library*

35,000. It actually rose a little after the end of the War, but there was a steady decline from 1956 onwards, and in 1976, there were only 2,100 looms operating in the town.

My brothers and I all served in the Forces in the Second World War, and were originally employed in textiles, but just two of us stayed in the industry until retirement. James began work at Haston Lee Mill at the age of fourteen and was employed there as a drawer and knotter until the mill closed in 1981. As an experienced worker he soon found employment with another company and stayed there until he retired in 1989.

After I left school at the age of fourteen, I began work with the British Northrop Loom Company as an apprentice loom fitter and after the war returned there until 1950 when I went to a mill in Rawtenstall working on loom maintenance. I obtained a Higher National Certificate and other qualifications in cotton manufacture and became a loom overlooker. The mill closed down in 1967 and I found a position at a mill in Blackburn and later became a shift foreman. This mill also had to close when the demand for their particular type of fabrics dried up. I was soon employed again by another manufacturer, but left them to become a shift manager at a recently re-opened mill which was specialising in a new type of furnishing fabric. Textile mills were closing at an even faster rate and the industry was in recession. After a few years this mill also closed down. At this time there were only about eight mills running in Blackburn but I was fortunate enough to be recruited by a manufacturer in Clitheroe where I remained until I retired in 1991.

Cotton had been king in Blackburn for over 150 years but its sad decline has almost annihilated the industry and, at the time of writing, there are just two weaving mills employed in the manufacture of cotton goods and these are producing specialised fabrics. From a peak of more than 94,000 looms at the end of the First World War, there are now about 100 looms only, operating in Blackburn.

My family's association with the textile industry, mainly in weaving, lasted for over 260 years consecutively, which coincided with the rise of Blackburn from a small market town, to being the core of a major industrial area.

Acknowledgements

I must acknowledge the assistance of the staff of the Lancashire Record Office, Blackburn and Accrington Reference Libraries, and Alan Duckworth, without whose help this article might never have been written.

3. CANAL BOAT BUILDING IN BLACKBURN

by Mike Clarke

THE LEEDS & LIVERPOOL CANAL finally reached Blackburn in 1810, forty years after the construction of the canal had begun. Seven boats were reported as sailing in procession from Enfield to Blackburn on the occasion of the opening; two children and three men fell into the water, and one man seriously injured his hand whilst firing a small cannon as the boats arrived at Eanam Wharf. For several months afterwards the Blackburn Mail reported the arrival of boats, just as if Blackburn was a great sea-port.

The final section of the canal, westward from Blackburn, was to take a further six years to complete, mainly due to problems with the embankments over the river Darwen and the Moulden Water, the latter being just beyond Feniscowles. However, the length from Riley Green to Wheelton was ready much earlier. As there were no boatyards there, a boat was sent by road to work on this section at the end of 1810. Sixteen horses pulled the boat on its eight mile journey, and even then it needed the help of the many onlookers to push the load up the steep bank from the Moulden Water, not really surprising as a Leeds & Liverpool Canal boat can weigh around fifteen tons.

Over the years, a number of boatyards were opened on the canal in East Lancashire. Burnley was probably the most important centre, with four boatyards operating around the town. In the second half of the nineteenth century, a small boatyard was situated at Church, close to the swing bridge there, but this seems to have closed in the 1870s. There was also a boatyard at Riley Green which continued to build wooden boats into the 1950s. Blackburn had two boatyards. One was at Whitebirk, the other at the drydock close to Paradise Bridge, now known as Eden Street, and from which Dock Street probably received its name.

Drydocks were relatively uncommon on the Leeds & Liverpool, boats usually being taken out of, or returned to, the water by means of side slipways. Drydocks could be found at Liverpool, Burscough, Parbold, Wigan, Blackburn, Burnley, Shipley and Leeds, while over twenty slipway sites were located along the canal. Today their remains are often difficult to find as the workshops have usually disappeared, though when you know where they were, it is sometimes possible to see the evidence of the slipways where they entered the canal.

A slipway comprised two parallel wooden rails, about thirty-five feet (10.75m) apart, which entered the canal at a slight angle, and on which baulks of timber slid. A boat was floated over the rails and the baulks of timber slid underneath. Hand-powered winches then pulled the wooden baulks up the rails and out of the water, the boat sitting on top of the baulks. Once out of the water, timber keel blocks were placed under the boat to spread the load and stop the boat from sagging in the middle. Very occasionally old boats became distorted in the water. If the centre had sagged they were called 'hogged', and if the ends had sagged they were called 'bobby-backed'. Such deformities could be rectified by use of jacks and strengthening when the boat was out of water.

The demand for boats - and thus boatbuilders - depended upon the volume of traffic on the canal. In 1851, following a period of competition, the carriage of general cargo was leased to a group of local railway companies who slowly ran down this traffic. They were not involved with the carriage of coal, grain and other bulk cargoes which continued to increase in volume. As one of the lessees, the Lancashire & Yorkshire Railway had a virtual monopoly in East Lancashire of the transport of general cargoes, and over the years their service, both on rail and water, declined in quality. By the early 1870s, local millowners and merchants had had enough and wrote to the canal company asking them to take back the lease from the railways. This was done in 1874, the canal company immediately setting about improving their service. By 1880 the Lancashire & Yorkshire Railway were having to lay off staff at Burnley because the canal had taken over much of their traffic.

Unfortunately, at first, there were insufficient boats to cope with the increased volume of traffic on the canal. Not only did the canal company ask all the existing boatbuilders to start constructing new boats, but they also set up two new yards, at Burscough and Blackburn. The second was at Whitebirk, where the boatbuilding yard of John Grimshaw was purchased for £150 in 1874. John Grimshaw owned Whitebirk Chemical Works which produced chemicals for the textile dyeing industry. The works included a bobbin turning shop and sawmill, and it was these that the canal company purchased, though Grimshaw may also have had his own boatyard on the site.

As soon as the purchase was made, the canal company leased the boatyard for 21 years to John Hodson, asking him to start building boats for them as soon as possible. John was then 54 years old and had been born at Tarleton. There were a number of boatyards there, and his father probably worked in one of them, subsequently moving to Burnley where he, and later John, worked as boatbuilders at the canal company's yard at Finsley Gate. It was in Burnley that John married and his two sons, Thomas and James, were born in 1859 and 1861. John must have been a reliable worker for the canal company to give him the opportunity to set up his own yard.

The Whitebirk boatyard was soon in operation, the canal company paying for a new saw pit and, after a few years, erecting a shed under which boats were repaired. This was replaced by a Belfast-roof in the 1920s. At first horse boats were built, but steam powered boats were introduced in the 1880s. The canal company's inspection boat *Waterwitch* was one of the first. Later in that decade Hodson's also built two unusual double-ended steam tugs for Foulridge and Gannow tunnels. As with all the steamers on the Leeds & Liverpool Canal, the engines were built by William Wilkinson of Wigan. Boats constructed at Hodson's had a good reputation. They were considered heavier than those built at Riley Green, but much sturdier, making them ideal for working into Liverpool Docks. Boats from Riley Green were usually built for carrying coal, and consequently did not get jammed between much larger craft as would happen in the docks. Hodson's did not just built cargo boats, but from time to time boats involved with the maintenance of the canal. These were either full size - around 60 feet (18.5m) by 14 feet (4.3m) - or somewhat smaller so that the bank rangers who maintained the canal could tow them easily by hand and so they were easier to pass when moored in difficult places.

John Hodson died in the mid-1880s, his brother William, also a boatbuilder, coming from Burnley to help John's sons keep the yard going. Besides boatbuilding, they would undertake any form of woodwork and local businesses soon came to rely upon them. Whitebirk Colliery, the chemical works and oil works, and Davies' knacker yard which took over the chemical works site around 1891, were all customers. Hodson's may have built and certainly repaired the horse drawn carts used by the canal company for deliveries around Blackburn.

By the time the lease of the boatyard ended in 1895 it had become a thriving business. Thomas and James purchased the site from the canal company, setting themselves up as T & J Hodson, the name under which the business continued until the end of traffic on the canal in the early 1960s. As with many canal families, not all the children went into the business. William Hodson's son John was a bookkeeper, and only John, Thomas' son born in 1884, and John Edwin, James' son born in 1887, are known to have worked as boatbuilders. John Edwin's son, also called Edwin and born in 1912, was the only one of his generation who worked at the yard, though daughter Mildred was one of the women, known on the canal as 'Judys', who worked on boats during the war to relieve the shortage of boatmen.

Although the boatyard was miles from the sea, the boatbuilders were knowledgeable about all aspects of boatbuilding. In fact, if they could build a canal boat, they had the ability to build or repair any other type of wooden boat. The vessels built at the yard were always known as boats, the term barge being applied to a flat-bottomed craft with a moulded beam or width of more than fourteen feet. This was measured across the outside of the craft's framing (not including the planking), and on wooden Leeds & Liverpool boats this was always just under fourteen feet. After serving their time in the yard, apprentices were always expected to work outside the area, becoming journeymen. Liverpool was the usual destination, and over the years

Figure 1. A turn of the century view of the *Alice* about to be launched at Whitebirk. It is a square-sterned, horse-drawn coal boat, possibly for Abner Brunskill who owned a similarly named boat in the mid-1870's. James Hodson is on the right, while next is Tom Brodson, a labourer at the yard, who holds a hammer over his shoulder. Jack Hodson (not J E Hodson) has his arm raised in the centre-left of the photo,while Bob Corson, a boat builder from Yorkshire who worked around Blackburn for many years, is fourth from the left. Note the highly decorative painting on the stern of the boat, which is typical of the Leeds & Liverpool Canal. This was the last boat to be built on the third slip at Hodsons, on the Blackburn side of the main covered slipway, whose shed is on the left of the picture. *Author*

several of the boatbuilders at Whitebirk had spent a few years working in Merseyside boatyards. A foreman shipwright at a Liverpool yard would always give a financial reward to the person who introduced a canal boat builder to his yard. As journeymen, boat builders could also work in the building trade learning more about carpentry, and the boatbuilders at Whitebirk were well able to take on any type of woodwork. (Figure 1)

At the end of the nineteenth century there were three slipways at Whitebirk. Two would usually be used for repairs, while the third was where new boats were built. At least three or four boats were built on average each year, while routine maintenance required boats to be slipped for a week or so every couple of years. There were usually four men working on each boat so, together with the work undertaken for local firms, there could have been around twelve men working for Hodson's at the start of the twentieth century. Some would have been local, such as William Hesketh who lived near Queens Park, whilst others came from other places along the canal, moving about as the opportunity for a better job arose. Jonathan Grimshaw, who worked at the yard around 1891, came from Accrington and may have originally worked at the small boatyard at Church. His wife and eldest daughter were born in Aspull, so he may have moved there after finishing his apprenticeship at Church. Wigan Coal & Iron Company certainly had a large boatyard at Aspull. Perhaps he took a job at Hodson's in order to move back nearer his old home.

Although the Leeds & Liverpool Canal Company were their main customer, Hodson's undertook work for local boat owners such as the Rishton Colliery Company who owned a fleet of around ten boats. They would also have built and maintained the grain-carrying boats working to Shackleton's and Appleby's East Lancashire mills. As these boats often had to cross the Mersey to load grain in Birkenhead Docks, the strongly-built Hodson's type would have been ideal.

During the First World War, traffic on canals was controlled by a government department. Maintenance was kept to a minimum and canals were handed back to their owners in a poor condition after the war. Unlike their railway competitors, canals were never fully compensated for their contribution to the war effort and the Leeds & Liverpool, along with several other canals in the north-west, sold off their general cargo carrying fleet in an effort to remain profitable. For about ten years Lancashire Canal Transport carried goods on the canal bound for East Lancashire, their successor, Canal Transport

Limited, keeping on the tradition until 1962. Hodson's built and maintained boats for both companies. They looked after the boats which carried coal from Burnley to the electricity power station at Whitebirk, built in the 1920s, and also the boats of local coal merchants.

Despite these developments, traffic on the canal declined after the First World War, and by the end of the Second World War the workforce at the yard had declined. Just one slip was in use then, though new boats continued to be built on the site of one of the other slips until the mid-1950s. In 1947, there were just five men and two apprentices working there. John Edwin Hodson, the son of James Hodson, was to remain in charge until boat repairs ceased in 1963. By then he was 75 years old. His son Edwin, who was in his thirties in 1947 was a boatbuilder, as was Walter Cooper, twenty years his senior. The workforce was completed by Irish boatbuilder Jack Shear and labourer Tommy Jones. In the early 1950s Clifford Sergeant, another boatbuilder, arrived. He had worked for forty years at the boatyard at Riley Green, but there had been a fire and one slipway had been destroyed. Clifford had lost his tools in the fire and after he was offered no compensation for them, had left to come to Hodson's.

Even after the war, Whitebirk remained a rural outpost of Blackburn. The Hodsons never seemed to have thrown anything away and, in this tranquil disorder, grass and wild flowers grew around their collection of old rudders, towing masts, horse lorries and assorted wooden items salvaged from old boats. Mice lived in profusion around the yard despite the attentions of two semi-wild cats which had made the place their home. Although the yard had a leisurely appearance, work started on the dot. No early-morning cup of tea to warm your hands before setting to work. The day started at a quarter to eight in the winter and finished at five with half an hour for lunch. In summer work started a quarter of an hour earlier and finished quarter of an hour later, but one hour was allowed for lunch. There was thirty minutes 'baggin' time' at ten o'clock, when a stop was made for a cup of tea and a sandwich, but there was no chance for such relaxation in the afternoon. There were also four hours to work on Saturday mornings, and annual leave was just five and a half days with six days Bank Holidays.

The original entrance to the boatyard was off the short road from the *Red Lion Inn* to the chemical works, a swing bridge extending the road across the canal. However, when Whitebirk Drive was built in the 1920s, access to the boatyard was down a short sloping path from the new road. The swing bridge was removed, but the narrows in the canal remained. It was the scene of summertime sports, with local pub teams having tugs-of-war across the canal, the losing team ending up with a soaking.

On entering the boatyard from Whitebirk Drive, the toilet, known as 'the tub', was on the left hand side. It was fitted inside a portable cabin, this being one of the many products of the yard. Being so near the road must have been a convenience for the night-soil men who came to empty the tub every week. There was a ram-shackle stable on the other side of the entrance which leant against the end of the saw mill, a long building erected when John Hodson took over the yard back in 1874. Originally timber was sawn by hand at the saw pit, but around the turn of the century a gas engine was installed in a shed at the end of the building. This drove a variety of machines: a large circular saw with a drag for pulling logs, a tilting band saw for cutting such items as the boat frames, a drill, grindstone and wetstone, the latter being used for sharpening tools. Later, after electricity had been installed, a mortising machine was purchased.

The floor of the saw mill was laid with old boat planks which covered the old saw pit. The pit was usually full of sawdust, and local children often came down for a bagful for their rabbit hutch. They liked to play in the pit, the darkness pierced by shafts of light from the gaps in the flooring, the dust swirling around in these beams of light. The children played in the pit until threatened with the boatyard's pet 'Buliphant', a ficticious beast thought up by Walt Cooper. The old hand saws used in the pit could still be found overhead, laying on the rafters, together with the moulds used for marking out the various frames needed to construct a boat. Templates made from yellow pine lined the walls. From these many of the jobs which had been undertaken at the yard could be identified: there were patterns for the wooden chimneys found on Yorkshire-built boats, patterns for wheelbarrows for delivering coal or those used by navvies, patterns for the knightheads which once graced the bows of canal boats, and patterns for felloes for making wheels. There were even patterns for chair rockers dating back to 1916 when they had made 200 of them at the yard. Nothing was thrown away, even if it was unlikely ever to be used again.

Outside, against the side of the saw mill nearest to Whitebirk Drive, was the drying shed; covered racking where soft-wood, used for joinery work, was stored in the dry. The fairing battens and spiling staffs, used for ensuring that everything was in line during construction or repair of a boat, were also kept in the drying shed. Extending the saw mill towards the canal was the 'peyark' or perch, racking made from old boat's timbers and against which any short pieces of spare timber were leant. If you needed wood for a small job, it was the first place you would look. Nearby the sawn baulks of English oak, the main timber used for boat building, were stored to season. After a tree trunk, often up to forty feet or more in length, had been sawn into flitches or planking, the 'slices' of timber were put back together with skids placed between them to allow the air to circulate and the oak to dry slowly. At every stage the timber was moved manually with levers, pinch-bars and the like.

New boats were usually built on the ground between the perch and the canal, while the covered slipway where boats were repaired stood on the left. Behind the Belfast roof which covered the slipway was the workshop. This was originally built by John Grimshaw and was probably where he made bobbins. There were several carpenters' workbenches, and in the corner closest to the road was the oakum hole. Oakum was the material used to caulk the seams between the planks of a boat to make it water-tight, and was made from treated hemp. (Today, old sacking, ropes and other such stuff are often the raw material.) In the nineteenth century, it used to be a job for prisoners to 'pick' oakum, breaking up the raw material into loose fibres. In the twentieth century it was delivered to the yard in bales, and everyone would be involved in rolling oakum to make the long strands which would later be hammered into a boat's seams.

The oakum hole was the only place in the boat yard where there was heating - an old cast iron range. It was where baggin' and lunch were eaten, the youngest apprentice having to brew up with water fetched from the boss's house. He also had to 'muck the bull', the phrase given to removing the ashes from under the range using a spade and barrow, a job done every month or so. Besides for making the tea, the stove was used for warming pies or making poached eggs in the lid of the cast iron kettle. Towards the end of a winter's day, when the light was too poor for work, the men would spend their time rolling oakum in front of the stove, getting it ready for the next caulking job. It was a chance for a warm job in winter. Many a yarn was spun to ease the boredom, with Irishman Jack Shear a past master at the art. Breaktimes in the oakum hole were filled with debate. Despite their basic education, the men at the yard were well read and had a lively interest in a wide variety of subjects. Many a time the flag floor would be covered with chalked diagrams as a particular problem was teased out. Paper was never used in the yard, and everything relating to work was written on planed pieces of wood called 'speaking chits'. This was exceedingly practical as paper would soon have disintegrated when working outside in wind and rain.

Next to the oakum hole was the darkest corner of the workshop, the sun never piercing this cobweb-bedecked gloom. Here lay dust-covered patterns for the cast iron parts used on a boat, such as those for bollards or for the various parts of a stove. Also left here were a pair of grappling irons, perhaps forgotten by the local police after they had used them for dragging the canal. At the other end of the workshop were several work benches, as well as an area large enough to assemble the five pieces of timber which formed one of a boat's frames. On the canal side of the workshop were the two winches, called cranes, which dominated the shop and were used for raising or lowering a boat on the slipway. These were wooden frames, each with a large cast iron hand-wheel over six feet in diameter. Hauling a boat out of the water was hard work for a small workforce, and men would be 'borrowed' from one of the other local firms to help turn the huge wheels. One time, wear on a gear shaft caused the gears to be forced out of mesh. One end of the boat started to slip back into the water with a tremendous crash which dislodged years of accumulated dust and dirt from the beams in the workshop and over the slip. One worker thought it was the 'crack o' doom'! It was only the speed of Edwin Hodson, who managed to release the other crane, which allowed the boat to slip safely back into the water without damage. It could take much of the morning to raise a boat out of the water, and the 'one down, one up' which the older men said was the normal work for a morning was never achieved in the 1940s or '50s. No boat was ever launched on a Friday as it was considered unlucky, while a shilling would be placed under the stern post when a boat was being built to ensure it had good luck.

At the eastern end of the workshop was the blacksmith's shop, where all the ironwork was produced. Outside was the cast iron base-plate from the old swing bridge which was used for levelling wheels, etc, while the crankshaft from the sawmill gas engine was set up for bending and rivetting chimnies. At the other end of the workshop was an extension forming the wheelwright's shop. Here repairs to horse-drawn vehicles were undertaken. Later, when petrol vehicles were repaired, it was called the body shop. Behind the workshop was the boiler. To bend the planks used to build a wooden boat which were two or three inch (50-75mm) thick, thirty to forty feet (9.25-12.3m) long and up to seven inches (180mm) wide, it was necessary to steam them. After the plank had been shaped, it would be placed in a long box into which steam from the boiler was fed. It took about

Figure 2. A drawing of a boatbuilder caulking a boat at Whitebirk in the 1940's or 50's. *Author*

an hour for each inch of thickness, and after the plank was ready it would be rushed to the boat, one end fixed and the plank carefully and swiftly bent around the frames.

When all the woodwork on the boat had been completed, it was then time to caulk the seams. On a Leeds & Liverpool canal boat there was around half a mile (0.8km) of seam to be caulked, and on a new boat it was usual to 'run in' three strands of oakum to each seam. This was no small job, and everyone in the yard had to help, and even the labourer, Tommy Jones, had learnt how to do the work. It was something which apprentices would only be allowed to do when they were at least eighteen or nineteen years old. The boat relied upon the oakum to keep out the water, so the caulking had to be done thoroughly, a boring and tiring job which required a mature mind (Figure 2).

After building or repairing a wooden boat, it was usual to fit ice plating to the bow as ice was sharp enough to severely damage unprotected wood. As part of the process the 'blear tub' would be brought out. 'Blear' was made from flocks which were teased out and mixed with thick gasworks tar, using a wooden paddle, in the blear tub. This was a wooden tub about three feet by one and a half feet by ten inches. The blear was applied to the back of the thin steel sheet used for the plating which was nailed onto the bow at the empty and loaded water line. The blear needed to be fairly soft to work properly, so in winter a 'controlled' fire would be lit in the tub to warm the tar.

After caulking, the seams had to be 'payed' with hot pitch which helped to hold the oakum and seal the joint. The pitch had to be mixed with creosote to achieve just the right consistency, and this always had to be checked by the boss. After heating the components, a piece of wood was dipped in the mixture, cooled in the canal and then taken to the office where it would be inspected. It was never rejected, but tradition had to be followed. Heating pitch and creosote was done over a fire of salvaged wood, and if there was a bit of water present, the mixture would froth up when the water boiled. If you were not quick enough to tap the side of the pot to control the frothing, it would boil over and the whole lot would go up in flames. Wet sacks had to be thrown over to put out the fire.

After the seams had been payed, a softer mixture of pitch and creosote was used to cover the outer planking. Then the real painting, called 'Brightwork', would be completed. Boats on the Leeds & Liverpool Canal had their own distinctive style which incorporated scrolls and other geometric shapes. Each boatyard had its own particular style, Whitebirk being noted for particularly artistic scrollwork, with fine curving lines. Although bright primary and secondary colours were used in profusion, the effect was not in the least garish. In the days of horse-drawn boats scenes would be painted on the ends of barrels used for storing drinking water, and a variety of old postcards and Christmas cards were kept to provide a guide. Inside the cabins, the panels were grained mahogany and oak, picked out in green.

When all the work had been carried out, the invoice would be made out in the office. In the 1950s, this was a portable cabin, another of the yard's products, located at the eastern end of the slipway. One end was under the Belfast-roof covering the slipway, so anyone in the office could keep an eye on work in progress both on the slip and outside. The office was lit by gas, and all the special tools, such as drills and augers, were kept there. The boss did all the book-keeping in the office, making up the wages for his workers, and in the evenings he sometimes returned to draw up technical details or the 'lines' for a boat, which record the shape of the hull (Figure 3).

So what was a day at the boatyard actually like? A boatbuilder, who worked at the yard for fourteen years briefly describes a typical winter's day during his first years as an apprentice:

I left the house at 7-15 to walk to work, a distance of about one and a half miles. The first half mile took me through streets swarming with clattering 'factory folk', just like some Lowry scene! The remainder of my journey took me through fields and by a meandering brook with just the sounds of the country to accompany me. The boatyard always felt close to nature and, on a board in one of the sheds, dates were written in chalk going back for years. These recorded

Figure 3. A view of the yard on a foggy day taken from the bypass bridge in the early 1950's. The slip had a Belfast roof by this time. One of the last boats built in the yard is in the foreground. The office, half in and half out of the slipway shed can be seen, together with the blacksmith's shop and, in the foreground, a variety of timber for building and maintaining boats. *Author*

the day in late February or early March when the first skylark had been heard each year. Its song told us winter was past.

Work began promptly at 7-45, and I usually worked with a leading hand or the boss himself. He was 62 years of age and had begun his apprenticeship in the late 1890s, learning the trade under the eye of his father and uncle. He was a self-educated and well-read person.. Although parsimonious, he was a fair and consistent man, and surely the finest craftsman I have ever known! All workmen at the yard were treated as one of the family, and on my trips to his house in Summerfield Terrace for drinking water for the yard, his wife would always expect to be kept up-to-date with happenings in my family.

Working conditions were poor by today's standards, especially in winter. Heating was almost non-existent, no running water, and the huge open shed offered little protection against driving rain, snow and the bitter east wind. However, workmanship was of the highest standard. Every man had a genuine quiet pride in his work. I recall no absenteeism, illness or latecomings, and 'come-backs' were unheard of.

Not just the craft of boatbuilding was carried out at the yard. A great deal of wheelwrighting, millwrighting, blacksmith's work and carpentry occupied much of the time. Hand tools were used constantly - the adze and drawknife in particular. On my return journey home, although physically tired, I invariably experienced an inner feeling of satisfaction, having both learned and created something that day. For three evenings, my work had not finished, and Mondays to Wednesdays in autumn and winter I attended evening classes at the college to learn maths, science and technical drawing, the latter being given by Mr. Lancaster, a knowledgable master carpenter and builder. On Thursday evenings I would visit the People's College in Whalley Range where lectures on subjects such as engineering, politics and architecture were given - though after the hard, open-air work, it was sometimes difficult to stay awake.

The boss made little acknowledgement of your hard work, but he never missed a thing. At the close of day he would call 'Show-up!', a traditional practice informing workmen that it was finishing-time. This custom originated two centuries ago when workmen, unable to afford all their own tools, 'showed-up' tools belonging to the firm.

The only time-piece at the yard was carried by the boss himself, a gold hunter complete with heavy gold chain and fob. On the one or two occasions when, at close of day, I happened to glance at this watch and commented on its fine porcelain face, the boss never responded to my remarks (Figure 4).

Figure 4. The yard in the 1970's viewed from the road entrance, when it was used by a caravan dealer. The old buildings can still be recognised, with the sawmill on the right and the workshop, smithy and slipway shed on the left. *Author.*

As the years passed I lost touch with the 'old man'. The boatyard gave way to a new motorway and the surrounding fields are now covered with car parks, DIY and other retail warehouses, while the brook,which formerly ran wild has been constrained in a perfectly straight concrete bed. The old boss died in his 85th year, thankfully unaware of all this 'progress'. But in his will he left me the gold hunter, chain and fob which I had admired all those years ago. Even now the watch can keep perfect time, yet it remains unwound, the hands at 5-15 - finishing time - 'Show-up' time.

4. THE BOROUGH OF DARWEN SPITFIRE

by Graham Groom

A LETTER APPEARED IN THE DARWEN NEWS for Friday 27 September 1940 from the town's Mayor, Councillor John Gregory, which began:

> *Sir, After careful consideration and following upon many requests, I have decided to open a local Spitfire Fund. It is desired to raise £5,000 for presentation to HM Government for the purchase of a spitfire. This sum may seem a very large amount to raise in Darwen, but so many towns have already raised much more than they had hoped, that I am constrained to believe that with the help of all sections of the community Darwen may very soon be afforded the pride and pleasure of offering the cost of yet another aeroplane for use by the RAF, in support of the great cause for which we are fighting.*

The Mayor appealed to everyone in the town; individuals, firms, companies and organisations to support the effort. He proposed that it should be known as the 'Darwen Spitfire Shilling Fund' and that a contribution should be in units of a shilling. He hoped that a contribution each week for a few weeks from every house in the borough would provide an excellent foundation for the fund.

The Mayor concluded that:

> *The Mayoress and I propose to open the fund with a contribution of 500 shillings and we are hoping for a ready and generous response for this appeal.*

Within the first two weeks of the appeal, £1,500 had already been raised. The Mayor called a meeting of the town's organisations to form a general committee to work out a scheme for raising the money. He emphasised that he wanted it to be a Darwen fund rather than a Mayor's fund. It was agreed that every effort be made to complete the scheme by the end of November, before the demands of Christmas.

The Town Clerk, Mr C C Byers, at the same meeting, praised the efforts already made by the small contributors, particularly the young, but emphasised that help was wanted from all organisations in the town.

A smaller sub-committee was formed out of the larger general committee to make further arrangements for the organisation of the fund.

It was stressed at that, and subsequent meetings that the large employers had done little towards the cause. It was felt there were many who could give £20, £50, or even £100. It was suggested that people be appointed to visit mills and works to ask for subscriptions and tell people it was their duty to make a donation. It was at this time that Mr J Taylor announced a gift of 5,000 shillings from the directors of R W Holden Ltd.

The Mayor later expressed the hope that they could go further than providing an aircraft, they could adopt a crew as well, including ground personnel, and provide them with cigarettes and other comforts.

At the next meeting of the sub-committee, Mr H Bradley, secretary of the Weavers' Association, suggested that employees and operatives of individual mills should subscribe weekly to their own collections, a minimum of sixpence being recommended for adults. It was further suggested that model spitfires be sold to children, who could then feel they were doing their bit to help the cause.

Mr A L Butterworth, manager of the Olympia Cinema, organised Sunday concerts, the first of which raised over £19. Efforts were also being made to bring a captured German aircraft to the town, to be displayed in the most central area available, with a small charge to be made for the privilege of viewing it.

As the weeks progressed, Spitfire fever hit the town. Money began to pour in as more and more events were organised. Over 300 people attended Holy Trinity School on Saturday 19 October 1940 for a whist drive and dance. Les Ainsworth and his Georgians provided the music, and the sum of £14 was raised.

Large contributions were being collected, such as the 5,000 shillings from the directors of India Mill, and the 439 shillings from their employees; the 2,100 shillings from the Darwen Paper Company; and the 1,000 shillings from Holden Haworth Ltd of Vale Rock Mill in Hoddlesden. The town's MP, Captain Stuart Russell, who was later killed in action, personally donated 210 shillings.

By 8 November 1940, 62,228 shillings and sixpence had been raised, with more coming in all the time. Two weeks later the total stood at 77,319 shillings, and by the following week 91,649 shillings had been raised. Donations were still coming in, ranging from just one shilling, up to 1,050 shillings from 'a Grocer and his Staff'. A mysterious contributor, known as 'X', contributed five shillings.

THE DARWEN SPITFIRE SHILLING FUND,

SPITFIRE SUBSCRIPTION LIST.

	Shillings.
Amount previous acknowledged	34,267½
Mr. G. Nutter	10
Mr. F. Vaughan	10
Mr. C. Harwood	10
"Lost and Found"	5
Mr. and Mrs. G. Whewell, 5, Victoria-street	20
Mr. and Mrs. Turner and Mrs. Kirkham, 5, Grimshaw-street..	30
Mrs. Grills, 93, Sudell-road, raffle	20
Mr. and Mrs. J. Thompson, 13, Alpha-street	21
E. D. Oldham, Market Hall, raffle	100
Mr. Hansell, Market Hall	5
Miss E. Haworth, 111, Avondale-road	20
Joyce and Philip Wrack, White-hall-terrace	15
Mrs. Nicholson, 64, Hollins Grove-street	5
Mr. J. Shipstone, 5, Elswick-st.	20
Miss D. Austin, "Woodlea"	40
Miss D. Knowles, 2, Broughton-street and Miss D. Prince, 25, Hindle-street	20
Mrs. Marsden, 22, Avondale-rd.	2
Mrs. Davis, 7, Park-road	2½
S. A. Mason, Silloth	1
Mrs. McCarrick, 34, Redearth-rd.	40
Three "B's"	1½
Anon.	5
Mr. and Mrs. J. E. Smith, 49, Hindle-street	10
Mr. and Mrs. A. Wilson, 1, Vernon-street	20
E.N.	5
M.D.	3
Kate and Martha	5
Mr. and Mrs. Harry Harwood, 101, Blackburn-road	500
Mrs. M. E. Berry, 53, Dove-lane	10
Mr. and Mrs. J. Fish, 71, Lyn-wood-avenue	10
Ivy Lowe, 22, Perry-street, and E. Fielding, 7, Perry-street	16
J. Fielding, Ltd., 169, Duckworth street, and 281, Bolton-road	105
Anon.	2½
Mr. and Mrs. T. Marsden, 5, Percival-street	10
Mr. and Mrs. J. G. Hibbert, Moorview	42
Mr. J. G. Hibbert, jr., Moorview	21
Woodfold Mill, raffle	21
Residents, Osborne-terrace	20
Mr. and Mrs. W. T. Taylor, 26, Hodgson-street	20
Mr. and Mrs. Gill, 5, Joseph-st.	100
Mr. and Mrs. J. L. Halliwell, "Heatherfield"	25
Mrs. and Miss Heap, 34, Ellison Fold-terrace	20
M.A.J., Dove-lane	2½
House-to-House Collection, Snape-street	33
Miss Elsie Kay, 8, Inverness-road, raffle	35
Workpeople, New Mill, 3rd contribution	45
Tom Knowles, 7, Gadfield-street, sale of tea-cosy	30
Mrs. Yates, Lytham	5
Lily Moss, 28, Joseph-street West	5
Edith Turbutt, 30, Joseph-street West	5
Billie Turbutt, 30, Joseph-street West	5
Master Jack Hayden, 22, Higher South-street	5
Mr. and Mrs. J. E. Thompson and daughters, 8, Belgrave-rd.	20
Mrs. W. Tattersall, 15, Snape-street, raffle	9
Mr. and Mrs. Almond, 55, Cemetery-road	10
Mr. and Mrs. Pearson, 36, Sandon-street	20
Misses Prior, "Newlands," Manor-road	60
A and I Bury Vernon-street	40

	Shillings.
Mr. and Mrs. T. Towers, 32, Brandwood-st. 2 old age pensioners	10
Mr. and Mrs. F. H. Cooper, 32, Queen-street	10
Mrs. Ellen Harwood, Scholes Fold, Pickup Bank	10
Coun. Mrs. Thompson and Mr. Thompson, 10, Belgrave-road	25
Workpeople and Staff, H. J, and A. Coulthurst, Ltd., 1st contribution	250
Mr. and Mrs. Wilkinson, 67, Heys-lane	21
Mr. and Mrs. H. Robinson, 305, Bolton-road	21
Master Colin Hodkinson, 197, Duckworth-st, 3rd contribution	10
M. Duprey, 26, Northcote-street	5
Mrs. E. Keys, 26, Northcote-st.	5
M. and H. Sharples, 40, Queen-street	40
Jane Morrison, 24, Melbourne-street, sale of d'oyleys	10
S. Smith, Home address, 90, Sudell-road, R.A.F.	2
Mr. and Mrs. A. Jannink, "Ellerslie"	500
Miss D. Scholes, 2, Somerset-avenue	2½
"Grateful," 2, Somerset-avenue	2½
Betty Fish and Mavis Ironfield, sale of d'oyleys	21
Mr. and Mrs. Killingbeck, 95, Duckworth-street	20
Darwen Golf Club	100
Mrs. E. Bradley, 61, Olive-lane, collecting box	30
Miss E. Brown, 4, Shaftesbury-avenue, and Miss D. Jepson, 2, Shaftesbury-avenue, raffle	16
R. Shorrock's men, Orchard Mill, per Mrs. Rawstron, raffle	17½
Mrs. Bucknall, 6, Lily-street	10
32, Longton-street	19
Mr. and Mrs. Aspinall, 1, Ellison fold-road	5
W. Sumner, jnr., 80, Greenway-st	12
Bowling Green Mill, per Mrs. Kirkham, raffle	75
J. Wild, 64, Redearth-road	21
Misses Bentley, 31, Baynes-st., Hoddlesden	20
Miss A. Greenwood, 90, Duckworth-street	10
W. A. Hacking, 17, Westminster-road	105
Mr. and Mrs. S. Wood, 50, Knowlesley-street	10
Mrs. Entwistle, 50, Knowlesley-street	10
Mr. and Mrs. D. Kelly, 5, Avon-dale-road	40
Master Donald Crompton, 83, Richmond-ter, d'oyleys	40
J.P., Lightbown Cottages	10
Mrs. Chadwick and Mrs. Shackleton, potato-pie effort	26
Mrs. Wilson, 29, Hope-street	15
Workpeople, H. Parkinson, Orchard Mill	11
Workpeople, B. Worsley, Ltd., raffle	23
Mr. and Mrs. T. H. Mather, "Newhaven"	500
Employees—India Mill (Darwen), Limited	181
Peaceful Valley	1
Mr. and Mrs. T. Entwistle, 6, Ratcliffe-street	25
Mrs. E. Hisom, 263, Blackburn-road, raffle of potato washer	60
	38,344½

CORRECTION to last week's list—
Mr. and Mrs. John Turner ... 400

Subscriptions should be sent to the Mayor's Parlour, or to the Borough Treasurer's Office

Everyone wanted to feel they were playing their part in the war effort.

The *Darwen News* recorded contributions (Figures 1 - 3) and was keen to keep patriotism on a high note. In the issue of 29 November 1940 it declared:

Every day gives further evidence of the invaluable work which is being done by spitfire planes in the defence of Britain. Let us give them another. And name it 'Darwen'. Your contributions are needed.

At a meeting of the Spitfire Fund Committee on Monday 9 December 1940 it was decided to close the fund the following Monday evening on 16 December. Over £5,500 had been collected. The Mayor announced that he thought Darwen had done magnificently, and that the townsfolk should be proud of the result.

It was also decided that exactly £5,000 be sent to the Government for the purchase of a spitfire and that the remainder be donated to the Air Force Benevolent Fund.

Mr Walter H Watson JP thought that this was an excellent idea and went on to say:

The Air Force Benevolent Fund is a most worthy cause, and I think we should make it known as widely as possible that all additional donations will be given to it. It may be that many who were not in agreement with the local Spitfire Fund may care to contribute to a fund which is concerned with the interests of the men of the Air Force.

SPITFIRE EFFORTS IN THE DISTRICT

Last week-end's figures:—

DARWEN	£3,111
Bacup	£3,007
Rawtenstall	£2,288
Oswaldtwistle	£2,054

DARWEN must keep the lead!
YOUR contribution will help.

Figure 2. Darwen's effort leading the way, Darwen News 15 November 1940. *Darwen Library*

Wardens' Spitfire Contribution.

£10 10s. FROM WHIST DRIVE.

A sum of about £10 10s. 0d. was raised for the Darwen Spitfire Fund as the result of a whist drive and dance, organised by the Wardens of Guard House "A", Blackburn-road, and held in the Hollins Grove Liberal Club on Tuesday evening.

About 120 people were present, and the event proved a most enjoyable one. Music for dancing was provided by Mr. G. L. Watson's orchestra, and Mr. Ben Whalley was the M.C. for whist and dancing. Refreshments were served during the evening, and Mr. J. Schofield, the chief warden, presented the principal whist prizes as follow:— Ladies: 1, Mrs. Heap; lady playing as gentleman, 1, Mrs. Pearson. Gentlemen: 1, Mr. Babbington.

Figure 3. The wardens' contribution, Darwen News 8 November 1940. *Darwen Library*

Figure 1. *(left)* List of subscribers to the fund, Darwen News 25 October 1940. *Darwen Library*

However at another meeting on 15 January 1941 it was decided that only £170 should be sent to the Benevolent Fund, and the rest forwarded to the Ministry of Aircraft Production. This change of heart was proposed by the Mayor himself after reading a letter in the *Darwen News* of 13 December 1940 which stated that as a matter of principle the majority of the money should go towards the Spitfire Fund.

The final total for the Fund, audited by John Adamson, Son and Co on 9 January 1941 appeared in the *Darwen News* for 17 January 1941: £6,008. 5s. 10d. had been subscribed, yielding, after the deduction of expenses, a net amount of £5,879. 19s. 11d.

The Mayor, in a letter in the same issue, expressed his thanks to all those who had contributed and closed by saying:

> *I am indeed deeply conscious of the exemplary spirit which has been displayed by the townspeople of Darwen in this nationally important cause which enables me to look forward with confidence to our meeting with fortitude and determination the sacrifices we may be called upon to bear for victory.*
>
> *We, of the many who owe so much to the few, will continue to strive to repay that great debt.*

Figure 4. The Darwen Spitfire. *Darwen Library*

Several days later Mr Eckersley, the Borough Treasurer, received a donation from a Miss Angela McDermott of Detroit, USA, of £25, which she had collected from other 'ex-Darreners' living in the city. She concluded her letter:

> *We all hope that this war will soon be over. We watch the news every day, and we all feel certain that we will win. So here is hoping that this donation will help a little. Maybe we will be able to do something else in the future.*

The final total of £5,707 was sent to Lord Beaverbrook at the Ministry of Aircraft Production on 1 February 1941. The Mayor asked if the aircraft could bear the name 'Darwen' and carry the coat of arms of the Borough. A positive response was received from Beaverbrook. A cheque for £171 was sent to the RAF Benevolent Fund at Hove in Sussex.

The spitfire was given the number VR7219 and was named the *Borough of Darwen* (Figure 4). It was received by the RAF on 26 March 1941 and allotted to 92 Squadron, then at Biggin Hill. After an air test on 7 April it carried out its first operation the following day:

a patrol of the Rochford area of Essex, flying at 15,000 feet (the famous 'Angels One-Five') in conjunction with 609 Squadron.

On 11 April 1941 it was one of four aircraft of a squadron detailed to destroy a seaplane being towed back to France by an enemy ship. The seaplane was sunk and the ship damaged despite attacks on the spitfires by Me 109's.

Twice the Darwen Spitfire was hit in action. The first time was on 27 May 1941 over France, but the pilot managed to land safely at Manston in Kent. On 16 June, along with another aircraft of the squadron, it helped to destroy two of the four Me 109's bagged by 92 Squadron whilst protecting a force of British bombers. Again it was hit, though the pilot managed to land at Hawkinge.

On 5 July 1941, after repairs, it was allocated to 74 Squadron at Gravesend. Three days later the aircrews were exchanged with those of 72 Squadron at Acklington. They took over each other's machines. The Darwen Spitfire remained at Gravesend, though it was now part of 72 Squadron.

On 14 July 1941, whilst on bomber escort duty over the Hazebrunck marshalling yard the Darwen Spitfire failed to return.

The life of the *Borough of Darwen* Spitfire was short, but not uneventful. 'Darreners' can be forever proud of their effort and can be said to have 'done their bit'.

5. The Lion of North Lancashire: William Beesley - Chartist

by William Turner

ON SUNDAY 4 AUGUST 1839, the Reverend J W Whittaker, vicar of Blackburn, preached a sermon in the Parish Church of St Mary to a congregation of some 4,000 people. A large congregation perhaps, but this was a special occasion (Figure 1).

The Blackburn members of a new political movement known as the Chartists had invited the Reverend Whittaker to preach that morning from the text James V 1-6 - 'Go to now, ye rich man, weep and howl for your miseries that shall come upon you'. The Chartists' motive was to entrap him into a public display of what they saw as the established church's hypocritical and reactionary attitude to the condition of the working people in the town.[1]

The Reverend Whittaker was in no mood to compromise. He began by welcoming the congregation to the house of God:

> *Where I believe most are perfect strangers-though I believe the party which has caused this unusual assemblage is contemptibly small and their leaders and instigators are no more than two or three dissolute persons whose characters are generally known.*[2]

Figure 1. Blackburn in 1851. In 1780 Blackburn had an estimated population of 5,000. Because of the rapid growth of cotton weaving this had risen to 36,000 in 1841. In 1851 it was 46,500. The population reached a maximum of 133,000 by 1911, after which the cotton industry, and the population, started to decline. *Blackburn Library.*

This set the tone of the sermon:

You are grossly deceived, most infamously and impudently deluded by persons who have their own wicked and selfish ends to answer by your destruction - you have excuses, one of these is your ignorance.[3]

He ended his sermon with an appeal, 'Come to church, but in humility, in penitence and faith. Finally, brethren, be patient in the Lord!'[4]

The words and tone of the Reverend Whittaker's sermon only confirmed to the Chartists present that the Established Church in Blackburn had no intention of facing the changes of a new industrial society where the development of the factory system and rapid urbanisation was bringing about deplorable living conditions for working-class families. The distress of unemployment, poverty and the horrors of the workhouse were made worse by the total lack of justice in the legal system. The two main political parties, the Whigs and the Tories, honestly believed the political system enjoyed the support of the country, and therefore no changes were necessary. The Established Church agreed.

Recent political reforms had not brought any benefits to the working classes. *The Reform Act* of 1832 gave the vote only to those who paid a minimum household rate of £10. In 1835 the vote was extended to all ratepayers. This again gave nothing to those who didn't own property. It was the *New Poor Law Amendment Act* of 1834, however, which caused much resentment among the poor. The Act established workhouses which were deliberately made unpleasant for the inmates to discourage people from asking for relief when unemployed or unable to support themselves: widows, children and the elderly.

Hatred of the workhouse and the inhumanity of the system was so fierce that it became one of the main causes of the rise of Chartism.

In 1837 six Radical MP's and six 'working men' (authors and journalists) presented a petition to the House of Commons which included the 'Six Points' which became the principles of the Chartist Movement. These were: universal male suffrage, equal electoral districts, annual Parliaments, payment for MP's, a secret ballot and no property qualifications for MP's. The six points were drafted into a formal Bill and entitled 'The Peoples Charter'[5]. This gave birth to the Chartist Movement in 1838 (Figure 2).

One of the Chartists in St Mary's Church was William Beesley, a Blackburn chairmaker. In 1839 he was twenty-seven years old and married with two children. He was the son of William Beesley, a chair-

The Chartists deliver a Bill to Lord John Russell, Prime Minister.

Figure 2. A cartoon of the time. Previous petitions were presented to Parliament on 14 June 1839 and 2 May 1842. This was the third and last, delivered by Feargus O'Connor on 10 April 1848. Lord John Russell was Prime Minister of the Whig government elected in 1847. *Author*

maker in business in Blackburn. At his father's shop at the corner of Northgate and Lord Street, William learnt his trade. Nearby, in Northgate, was the *Holy Lamb* public house (later the *Stanley Arms*). In May 1839, after twenty-six years in business, Beesley the elder moved into premises behind the *Holy Lamb*.

The *Holy Lamb* was on the 'tramping route' of journeymen artisans, where a craftsman travelling the country seeking work could have a bed for the night or be hired for a job[6]...

As all journeymen were members of trade associations (early trade unions), the *Holy Lamb* was the haunt of democrats and radicals. It is feasible that here William Beesley developed his radical philosophy.

The first known reference to William Beesley in the newspapers was in July 1839. During that month a meeting of the 'Democrats of Blackburn' was held in the Music Hall. The local Chartists must have been numerous enough for Feargus O'Connor, the national leader of the Chartists, to accept an invitation to speak. He was however, unable to attend (because of the arrest of other Chartist leaders in Birmingham) and at the invitation of the chairman, Mr Mickle, a bookseller of King Street, Beesley spoke instead.

The tone of his speech was inflammatory to say the least. He was reported as saying:

> *If the rights of the people are much longer withheld bloodshed and anarchy must inevitably follow.*

He ended, however, on a note which drew laughter from the audience. In appealing for a general strike, he said 'The colliers should stop working and then the chimneys would stop smoking and then where would the tyrants find themselves?'[7]

On 12 August 1838, only six days after the Reverend Whittaker's admonitions, an unrepentant Beesley addressed a Chartist meeting at Rising Bridge. The editor of the *Blackburn Standard* was in the crowd and reported the event in a mocking and derisory tone. Beesley's speech, notwithstanding, was violent in tone:

> *Never, until every man is possessed of arms will we obtain our rights. When every man is armed the Government will give way.*

On seeing the journalist Beesley launched into a 'violent tirade against the abominable and vicious press'.[8]

The appeal to arms was Beesley's undoing. He was later arrested on a charge of sedition. On 23 March 1840 at Lancaster Assizes, he was found guilty. For what was a hanging offence he got away lightly when he was bound over to keep the peace in his own recognizance of £100.

We know little of Beesley's activities in 1840, although the binding over order would have had some effect. The year ended on a high note, however, in a way which gives some idea of his devotion to his chosen cause. He wrote to the *Northern Star* to say that he,

> *Pledges himself to abstain from all snuff, tobacco and intoxicating drink until the six points of the Charter are achieved*[9]

He appealed to others to follow his example. The decision would not be a difficult one for Beesley. He was a highly moral family man with a Methodist background so it was no coincidence that he made temperance a feature of Blackburn Chartism. Committee meetings were held in the *Temperance Hotel* Darwen Street. Beesley was also, unique in his day, an advocate of equality for women. He forbad meetings in public houses because this would have prevented women attending (only the lower sort of women frequented public houses).

Throughout 1841 Beesley addressed scores of Chartist meetings and set up new branches all over the district of North Lancashire. He was by now becoming known for his oratory and the passion for which he spoke for the Charter. He didn't hesitate to use extreme and colourful language. In a speech at Lancaster on 28 September 1841 he condemned the Tories to perdition and said he would rather go to the bottomless pit to take up one of the vilest imps to send to Parliament sooner than vote for a Tory. No corrupt government would ever put him down, for he would stand up as the advocate of liberty to his last hour. He was loudly cheered at the conclusion, as well as frequently during his excellent speech.[10] His popularity was such that he was soon delegated, as the representative for North Lancashire District, to the National Convention of the Chartist Movement in London in April 1842. He still had his enemies, however. On 1 July 1841, which was voting day in the General Election, there was a lot of riotous behaviour amongst supporters of the candidates in Blackburn. During that day Beesley was arrested on a charge of being concerned with a violent incident outside the *Black Bull* public house. Several witnesses swore to Beesley's presence. He was remanded until Saturday 3 July in order to get more evidence. Witnesses were then called to state that Beesley was in Mr Burrell's Newsroom at the time. The evidence was so contradictory that the magistrates dismissed the charge.[11]

In the early months of 1842 Beesley continued his work as a speaker and organiser. In a somewhat punishing schedule, on ten consecutive days in January, he spoke at Chorley, Wigan, Preston, Clitheroe, Sabden, Barnoldswick, Colne, Burnley, Todmorden and Bacup.

At the National Convention in April, he presented a petition of 52,000 names from the North Lancashire district. He also played a full part in the debates. In the nearest we have to a description, a London newspaper was quoted as saying that:

Beesley, he with the leonine head and sonorous voice, had an unsurpassed gift of oratory. He was repeatedly applauded with a degree of enthusiasm seldom seen in London.[12]

His success at the Convention made him a local hero. In Burnley on 10 May more than 4,000 people assembled in the Market Place to hear him speak. Later, in Blackburn, he spoke to a packed Music Hall where he was given a 'splendid reception'.

The Blackburn magistrates, however, had had enough of Beesley. On 19 August 1842 they wrote to the Home Secretary giving an account of the 'plug drawing riots' in the area. (The terrible distress in Blackburn, plus Parliament's rejection of a second Chartist petition for reform, led to many strikes and outbreaks of violence. Mills were stopped from working by gangs removing the boiler plugs). The magistrates added:

> *We should be exceedingly happy to hear of the seizures of the persons and papers of some of the Chartist leaders. There is one of the name of Beesley who is a pest of society and ought, in our opinion, be committed to prison. We understand he is skulking about in disguise.*

The Home Secretary, in his reply, succinctly pointed out that a person had to violate the law before he could be sent to prison. It was not enough to be a pest.[15]

The magistrates were wrong about Beesley. Firstly, he was opposed in principle to the plug drawing riots and secondly, he was in Newcastle at the time.

Possibly invited at the National Convention, Beesley spoke at a number of Chartist meetings in the North East during August. He spoke 'in a very eloquent style' to a meeting in Newcastle and went on to Gateshead, North Shields and Morpeth. On his way to Morpeth he was stopped by a group of men who asked him to address an impromptu meeting of 200 miners. This was to be the beginning of a new career for Beesley.

Beesley went back to the North East a month later and, his reputation growing, was also invited to speak to a meeting in Sheffield. The *Northern Star* reported 'three times three tremendous cheers for the Lion of North Lancashire' followed the conclusion of his lectures. All present were highly delighted'[14].This was the first reference to 'The Lion of North Lancashire' - a name which stuck to him for the rest of his Chartist activities. Although he continued his tour of the North East, he still spoke at venues throughout Lancashire, including Accrington, where he lived (Figure 3).

Meanwhile, in September 1842, the Government, alarmed at the popularity of the Chartists, arrested Feargus O'Connor and 58

Figure 3. This shop in Abbey Street was William Beesley's first home in Accrington. His wife kept it as a coffee house and reading room for Chartists, so it is appropriate that this photograph, taken at the end of the century, shows advertisements for hot drinks. *Accrington Library*

others. Among them was Beesley. He was detained on 10 September at the *Temperance Hotel* in Burnley on two charges of sedition (at Pendle Hill on 12 June and at a similar meeting at Whinney Hill, Clayton-le-Moors, on 29 June) and having in his possession several copies of a resolution passed at a conference at Manchester, which was deemed to be seditious. He was then bailed on his own recognisance to appear at Lancaster Assizes on 7 March 1843.

In the trial Beesley conducted his own defence in which he said he opposed the turn-out (strike) which led to the Plug Riots with all his might. He could not, therefore have conspired with anyone to create a revolution or rebellion. He believed he had been arrested simply for being a Chartist.

He told the court,

*A Chartist I am and whatever amount of persecution or imprisonment
that I be subjected to, I will remain a Chartist. Let 10,000 convictions
be obtained against me I will be a Chartist still.* [15]

With these defiant words he ended his defence.

Of the defendants, including Beesley, thirty-one were found guilty,
with several going to prison. Again Beesley got off comparatively
lightly: he was given a conditional discharge for twelve months. The
trial, however, had the effect the Government had hoped for. With
many of their leaders in prison, membership of the movement
plummeted and its activities were severely curtailed.

It must have been clear to Beesley that the police, magistrates and
press in Blackburn were determined to put an end to his activities.
Because of this, in December 1842, he accepted an invitation by the
Northumberland and Durham Miners Association to become their
District Lecturer. After the trial, he left for the North East. He spent
the Spring and Summer of 1843 speaking to Chartist meetings and
gatherings of miners.

On 11 August 1843 the Miners Association of Great Britain, at a
meeting in Newcastle, appointed a barrister, William Prowting
Roberts, as their legal advisor. Roberts was a leading Chartist and he
was the first lawyer to campaign for worker's rights. Beesley's
contacts, and his talents, were invaluable to someone like Roberts.
On 12 September Beesley was appointed as Roberts' solicitor's clerk.
His salary was £140 a year.

At that time all coalmine owners decided their miners' pay and
conditions of employment. This was the 'Bond'. It was a tyrannical
system where wages could be deducted for little or no reason, and
where men were imprisoned for refusing to accept the conditions of
the Bond. Immediately Roberts started to defend miners in court
and began to win case after case. [16]

Beesley's job was to interview and advise aggrieved miners and
prepare cases for Roberts. He also assisted Roberts in court,
occasionally presenting cases himself in Roberts absence. In this
work Beesley shared with Roberts the approbation in which miners
held his legal victories in their cause. On 14 October 1843, for
instance, Beesley shared the platform with O'Connor and Roberts at
a rally of 30,000 miners and their families at Sheddon Hill, near
Newcastle.

Beesley also took on another job. He became the editor of the
Miners' Journal, set up by Roberts to publicise legal developments
relating to the coal industry. The *Northern Star* of 28 October 1843

was generous in its comments:

This is a publication devoted to the interests of the miners conducted by a well known advocate of the democratic principle, Mr William Beesley. Mr Beesley's sterling honesty and his notorious steadiness of character are sufficient guarantees for the uncompromising spirit in which this publication will be conducted.

Beesley's star was in the ascendant.

In the summer of 1845 Roberts became the legal advisor to the Lancashire Miners' Association. This, of course, meant more work for Beesley. He subsequently shared his time between the North East and Lancashire, visiting striking miners to advise them of their rights and obligations. He spoke, in this way, to miners at Hapton, Chorley, St Helens, Patricroft, Eccles and Worsley. Each time he attempted to end the strike on amicable terms. If this failed, he prepared a report for Roberts who then took the employers to court. In this way they worked together throughout 1844 and 1845. (The pressure of work forced Beesley to relinquish the editorship of the *Miners' Journal*).

Not all, however, looked at Beesley in a favourable light. On 25 December 1844 his old enemy, the *Blackburn Standard*, said in an editorial,

The cause of discontent existing amongst the colliers in Lancashire does not occur from the fact of their being exposed to distress or oppression, but from the mischievous promptings of designing schemers who make a handsome living out of the strife they stir up between masters and men.

(Who else but Beesley and Roberts?).

Meanwhile, the miners of Northumberland and Durham were out on a general strike. The strike lasted until August 1844, when they returned to work defeated. Their Association virtually ceased to exist. Although Roberts stayed in the area and worked virtually unpaid, Beesley, perforce, had to return to his home in Abbey Street, Accrington. This change of fortune meant that, although still working for Roberts in Lancashire, he needed another income. He set up in business as an auctioneer and returned to his trade as a chairmaker. He involved himself in more local affairs.

Beesley worked for Roberts throughout 1845, 1846 and 1847. In a celebrated case in June 1845 in a strike by miners at Messrs Simpson's, Broadfield Colliery, Oswaldtwistle, against the bondage system, Roberts took the case to the High Court. He proved that a miner under the age of twenty-one was a 'minor' and as the employer had not first asked his mother's permission, his bond was illegal. (Under the law anyone under the age of twenty-one was defined as an infant). This case helped bring about the end of the bondage system in Lancashire.[17]

Through Beesley's influence Roberts also acted on behalf of striking powerloom weavers at Hopwood's mill in Blackburn in May 1847. Roberts won the case on a legal technicality, but the weavers lost the strike. The millowner, Robert Hopwood, happened to be the Returning Officer for the Blackburn constituency. His weavers, disgruntled at their defeat, decided to express their displeasure. At Beesley's suggestion the Weavers' Association proposed Roberts as the Chartist candidate in the forthcoming general election in Blackburn. Although they themselves did not have the vote, they wanted to both advance their cause and also show how undemocratic the electoral system was. Beesley was proposed as Roberts' running mate, but he thought it best to concentrate all possible votes on Roberts.

In the ensuing election campaign, however, Beesley occasionally deputised for Roberts if he was engaged on work elsewhere. Both Beesley and the *Blackburn Standard* ran true to form:

> *We notice a most wicked and dangerous attempt on the part of one of the speakers, named Beesley, to incite his hearers to a riotous act upon the Returning Officer, Robert Hopwood. This man declared to the thousands assembled round him that Mr Hopwood was abominated, hated and detested - and if he dared to show his face during the election there would sure to be a riot'*[18]

Whether one, or both, were exaggerating is not known, but the *Blackburn Standard* clearly detested Beesley and all he stood for.

On polling day thousands gathered at the hustings at which the candidates spoke. For the first time ever voteless workers were not supporting their employers' choice, but their own. Roberts, more eloquent than the others, was the hero of the hour as he expounded Chartist principles. The result, of course, was a foregone conclusion. A local man, John Hornby, (Tory) with 641 votes, and James Pilkington (Liberal) with 601 votes, were elected. Roberts' share was a paltry 68. Although he was soundly defeated, he was the first election candidate ever to be sponsored by a trade association or union.

The rejection by Parliament in April 1848 of a third Chartist petition signed by over five million people, saw the beginning of the end of the Chartist Movement. Many became disillusioned and membership further declined. Although Beesley continued working for Roberts during 1848 and 1849, it is clear he was no longer an active Chartist.

In March 1846, a fellow Chartist and friend, John Julian Harney, formed the Fraternal Democrats, a society concerned, amongst other things, with the labour movement in Europe. Beesley became a member in November 1847. His special interest was in the Committee for Polish Regeneration, a movement committed to democracy ih Poland.

On 29 November 1847, at a meeting of the Fraternal Democrats, Karl Marx spoke for the first time to an audience of British democrats. Marx met the Fraternal Democrats and similar organisations several times whilst he was writing the Communist Manifesto, and he was anxious to exchange ideas. It is known he was much influenced by the Fraternal Democrats.

Like many former Chartists, Beesley had gifts of oratory, of organisation and a firm belief in democracy, he put these talents to the benefit of the township of New Accrington. On 25 November 1849 he was present at a meeting of ratepayers to appoint Lighting and Watching Inspectors. He took an active part in subsequent meetings. On 29 August 1853 he was appointed Clerk to the Lighting and Watching Inspectors and also Superintendant of the Fire Brigade, with a remit to appoint twelve men as firemen (Figure 4). His salary

Figure 4. This request for firemen's wages, to the Treasurer of the Township, is dated 1 April 1854. This would be part of his duties as Superintendent. After February 1855, rather strangely, there is no reference to him in the minute books. *Accrington Library*

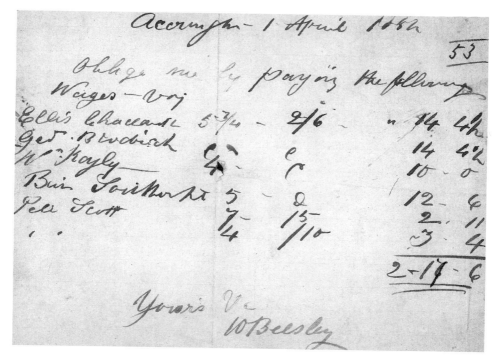

was eight shillings a week.[20] (It is clear he had changed very much since his days of seditious and violent speeches).

At a Township meeting at the *Red Lion* public house on 5 February 1855, it was resolved that 'The accounts be passed as produced by William Beesley'. (His salary was then twelve shillings a week). Also minuted, was an item, not unfamiliar in the 1990s,

> *That the Superintendent be instructed to reduce the number of men as to make the amount of money now on hand to meet the expenses of the current year.*

This is the last known reference to Beesley.[21]

The final chapter of Beesley's life is surrounded in mystery. Sometime after this meeting he disappeared. He was last seen one night near the Town Hall. (Perhaps it was not a coincidence that his old Chartist friend, Thomas Tattersall, had his bookseller's shop next to the Town Hall).

From now on all is speculation. Beesley's life was such that there could be many reasons for his disappearance. There were also many reasons why he should stay. He was a family man, a teetotaller, he was in business, he had a good position with the Township, his accounts there were in good order: all the signs of a settled life.

He would certainly have political enemies, but he was hardly the sort to run away. As a Fraternal Democrat, he may have visited Europe, or had contacts there. In an age of no passports, it would be easy to travel abroad under an assumed name. If he did, why? Did he live a double life? Was he murdered? Whatever the reason, it remains a fact that he disappeared completely.

Beesley was certainly a gifted and a courageous man. He had a wide range of interests and was eminently literate. He was a true radical and democrat. This leads one to a further speculation.

It is extremely likely that Beesley was the type to whom Karl Marx spoke on his visits to England. It may be possible Marx was influenced by some of Beesley's ideas. Beesley would certainly be forthright about them. It may - or may not - be a coincidence that Helen Macfarlane, the sister of William Macfarlane, a calico printer of Bridge End, Burnley, was the first translator into English of the Communist Manifesto. She was a friend of Marx and Harney, an active Chartist known to Beesley, who also lived at Bridge End.

It may be, therefore, that Beesley, if only in a peripheral way, was involved in the very beginnings of what later became the world-wide political movement of Communism. If so, this would be but one of the achievements of the courageous, outrageous, enigmatic William

Beesley - Blackburn chairmaker, Chartist and 'Lion of North Lancashire'.

Notes and References

1. The invitation was issued to other churches in the area but none took it up. In Haslingden, for instance, the Reverend William Gray, vicar of St James', declined, saying the passage was not relevant to their times but to a special period in Jewish history.

2. The Church and the Chartists in Blackburn, Blackburn, 1839. (Booklet reproduced by Blackburn Cathedral 1972) p18.

3. Ibid p18

4. Ibid p22

5. It is difficult today to appreciate the passion the Charter generated. To the working classes it was not just a political creed but the hope of salvation; to the gentry and the middle classes it smacked of revolution. Those who preached Chartism were feared and detested.

6. Leeson, RA, Travelling Brothers', Granada, 1980 - for a detailed description of the system.

7. The Northern Star, 13 July 1839 (Published in Leeds, it was the newspaper of the Chartist Movement).

8. Blackburn Standard, 14 August 1839.

9. Northern Star, 26 December 1840.

10. Ibid, 2 October 1841.

11. Miller, George C., Blackburn : The Evolution of a Cotton Town, reprinted by THCL Publishing, Blackburn, 1992.

12. Quoted in the Northern Star, 1 May 1842.

13. HO 45/249, Public Records Office.

14. Northern Star, 29 October 1842.

15. The Trial of Feargus O' Connor - and fifty-eight others at Lancaster on charges of Seditious Conspiracy, Tumult and Riot, Manchester, 1843, p266.

16. See Challinor, Raymond, A Radical Lawyer in Victorian England, IB Taurus, 1990, for a detailed description of Roberts' and Beesley's work.

17. Blackburn Standard, 2 July 1845.

18. Ibid 2 June 1847.

19. Northern Star 12 December 1847.

20. Minute Books Lighting and Watching Inspectors, New Accrington 1849-1853, Accrington Local Studies Library.

21. Minute Book of Ratepayer's Meeting, Township of New Accrington, 1855, Accrington Local Studies Library.

6. BLACKBURN AT THE POLLS: ELECTIONS AND POLITICS IN THE TOWN'S HISTORY

by Matthew Cole

Blackburn does not like strong meat
Comment of *Northern Daily Telegraph*'s AG Gardiner
on the candidature of Philip Snowden in 1900

POLITICS IS OFTEN REGARDED AS a regrettable intrusion into everyday life, and not always without reason: certain politicians of our own generation have done little to enhance the reputation of their colleagues. The people of Blackburn, as AG Gardiner (who went on to achieve national prominence as Editor of the *Daily News*) testified, are as sceptical as most about political promises. Nevertheless, a town's voters, activists and leaders can tell the onlooker a good deal about other aspects of its history - news that is sometimes welcome, sometimes unhappy; whether about stuffy reactionaries, hot-headed troublemakers or the disillusioned, long-suffering public. The story of Blackburn's elections and power struggles over the last two centuries reflects important truths about both the town's character, and the role of its MPs in national politics. Most of that news, happily, is good.

Before 1832: Politics without Elections
Prior to the *Great Reform Act* of 1832, Blackburn, like many areas which grew with the industrial revolution, had no representatives of its own in Parliament. However, tempting as it might be to believe that political argument was invented by MPs, it went on long before they arrived. Decisions about public life in Blackburn before 1832 were made by a mixture of landowners, churchmen, courts and employers.

Between Cromwell's Commonwealth and 1803, when twelve police commissioners were appointed, everything from recruiting soldiers to tackling local nuisances was handled by nine or more members of the parish vestry, who appointed a Petty Constable. In a town of fewer than 12,000 souls, whose public life was concentrated in the tight area around the old market cross, this was enough in the way of government. More serious or particular matters would be the business of other authorities: Overseers managed the workhouse; churchwardens collected local rates; officials of local charities provided schools. Market trustees implemented regulations imposed from Parliament about trade; law and order were maintained by the magistrates, the keepers of the House of Correction in Darwen Street, if necessary supported by the High Sheriff and troops called in from the barracks in King Street.

Since Elizabethan times, certain public functions had been carried out by Freeholders of the town, of whom there were 185 by 1820. The patchwork of these arrangements was further complicated by the division of the rights of the Lord of the Manor from 1721 to after 1800 between the Baldwin, Sudell and Feilden families.

As Blackburn began its spectacular growth and development, this limited framework became increasingly evidently inadequate. A town of nearly 30,000 inhabitants, growing by up to 10,000 each decade, had no council, no MPs, and therefore no means of resolving the myriad controversies which the rapidly changing circumstances threw up. Without democratic machinery, and trade unions being outlawed for the first quarter of the nineteenth century, public opinion was at times of crisis expressed through direct action. Farmers and provision dealers were attacked in 1800 and 1808 in protest at high food prices; in 1818, 4,000 weavers waving the French revolutionary tricolour marched from Blakey Moor to the home of cotton magnate Henry Sudell at Woodfold Hall to demand a pay rise. Eight years later, a spate of violence involving attacks upon the carriages of millowners and the home of the JPs clerk, culminated in a pitched battle around Salford Bridge and Darwen Street between a mob of up to 10,000 aiming to destroy power looms, and soldiers who had followed them from Accrington. The rioters, armed with pikes, sledgehammers, and guns, raided *The Bay Horse Inn* in at the foot of Furthergate, and eventually smashed the looms in town centre mills before the *Riot Act* was read and troops opened fire.

It is easy to see why in 1832 members of all social groups in the town warmed to parliamentary reform: it was, after all, the new industrial elite whose property was under threat from such disturbances, and who were themselves sometimes called upon, as cavalry and infantrymen of the Volunteers, to risk more than their property. Thus, when in 1830 Lord Grey's Whig government proposed a review of parliamentary representation, the plan was initially supported with enthusiasm by the radical, working-class Blackburn Political Union, led by George Dewhurst. Even when details of the limited changes were published in May 1831, Dewhurst argued that 'simply because we cannot attain all of what we want ... we ought not to refuse partial reform'. However, a year later, he was calling for petitions against Parliament and the King for their alleged betrayal of the country's demands for reform. As he suspected, the new system was not to be a democratic one - but nor was it to be entirely unsuccessful from the point of view of Blackburn's fortunes.

1832-1906: Liberals, Tories and King Cotton

Throughout the nineteenth century, Blackburn's voice in parliament was the voice of local entrepreneurs - almost always millowners. The privilege of representing the town was restricted to a coterie of well-connected businessmen. It was a privilege they defended fiercely, and not always fairly.

The first election set the pattern clearly: in it, four contenders were nominated publicly at the hustings for Blackburn's two seats in the Commons. The names of three of these - William Feilden, William Turner and John Fowden Hindle of Woodfold Hall - are synonymous with property and textiles in Blackburn; the fourth, Liberal scholar John Bowring (Figure 1), was defeated after Hindle withdrew on the eve of poll to assist his Tory stablemate Feilden, and Turner, a Whig, used what were later politely referred to as 'local influences' to sneak ahead of his opponent on the latter of the two days' poll. Turner and Feilden became the first of fourteen textiles magnates to represent Blackburn in Parliament out of a total of fifteen MPs. Just to complete the picture, the Returning Officer in 1832 was none other than John Fleming, the cotton merchant who established a cloth hall in the square which still bears

---

BLACKBURN SONG
OF FREEDOM.

Tune.—" Scots, wha ha."

Come and join in freedom's song !
Be our voices bold and strong,
Be our triumph loud and long,
        Worthy of the free !

Leave corruption to the base !
For our country—for our race,
In our hearts a resting place—
        Freedom's shrine shall be.

Worthy of our Sires' renown,—
We have hurl'd oppression down,
And we wear the laurel crown,
        Green with victory.

Ours the pure and emerald bow,
Green of spring and white of snow,
Honoring lofty, honoring low,
        Dear to liberty !

We the brave Blackburnian band,
Warm in heart and strong in hand,
Who shall daunt us—who withstand ?
        Cowards—tyrants flee !

They who freedom's smiles deserve,
Never from her counsels swerve,
They can suffer,—they can serve,
        Firmly,—faithfully !

Every triumph that we gain,
Shall our free born sons maintain,
And establish freedom's reign,
        Everlastingly !

            JOHN BOWRING.

J. Burrell, Printer, Blackburn.

Figure 1. 'Blackburn Song of Freedom', this was the rousing anthem sung to fife and drum by supporters of liberal scholar John Bowring, who was narrowly defeated in 1832 and 1835. *Author*

his name, and the Chairman of the victorious Tories was cotton manufacturer WH Hornby.

Moreover, these were industrialists with a thorough local pedigree, and outsiders were given short shrift by Blackburn's electors. Bowring's extensive travels abroad were regarded with suspicion by Tory paper the *Blackburn Alfred*, which warned he had 'surreptitiously contrived to set himself upon us'. He was only the first in a series of noted visitors to the town to be snubbed at the polls in favour of less celebrated natives. John (later Lord) Morley, though raised in Blackburn, was an Oxford scholar and edited the *Fortnightly Review*, keeping company with the likes of John Stuart Mill, before he came bottom of the poll in his home town in 1869; in a by-election of 1875, the well-known former MP for Oldham JT Hibbert, was rejected despite the *Blackburn Times'* rhetorical appeal 'are Oldham and Blackburn so far apart in physical distance that he who is closely associated with the one town should be regarded as a stranger by the other?' W H 'Harry' Hornby is famed for resisting the lure of London so hard that he never spoke in Parliament in twenty-three years as Blackburn's MP, and in 1895, TP Ritzema, editor of the *Northern Daily Telegraph*, was thwarted in his attempt to remove Hornby partly because of doubts about his local loyalties as a man who had only ten years earlier moved to Blackburn from Darwen!

The only local MP before 1900 without substantial investment in land and factories in Blackburn was Robert Peel, son of the former Prime Minister, and grandson of the famous Blackburn manufacturer, who represented the town for seven months.

These local men were more than employers - they were celebrities of a sort, too, surrounded by a folklore which modern PR agents might struggle to cultivate for their clients. Turner briefly hit the national news in 1826 when his daughter was abducted to Gretna Green and thence to Calais by a duplicitous lover who was later imprisoned. Liberal WE Briggs, Blackburn's MP from 1874-85, was feted for the victory of his dog 'Bed of Stone' in the 1872 Waterloo Cup, and was later described by George Miller as 'the only member who ever entered that August House on the back of a greyhound'. Sir John Rutherford, Blackburn's Mayor in 1888, and MP for Darwen for 27 years, invested in racehorses, his colt 'Solario' winning the St Leger. He and other Blackburn politicians were also given to staking sizeable public wagers upon their reputations when accused of making contradictory promises. Even the relatively coy William Coddington, sardonically dismissed in a contemporary profile as 'a better print-maker than a politician', sought to add colour to his public image by

Figure 2. W H Hornby from a privately commissioned book by the Hornby family recording their remarkable contribution to Blackburn's public life.
Author

taking the last carriage to pay a turn-pike fee out of Blackburn on the turnpike road to Preston in 1890. Such was the self-esteem of the Hornby family that in 1892 they commissioned Blackburn historian William Abram to write a privately published edition of a glowing account of their contribution to politics in the town (Figure 2). Such flamboyance, if sometimes forced, is something which Blackburn has expected of its MPs ever since.

Another tradition which survived the arrival of electoral politics in Blackburn was the influence of the Church of England. For more than two decades following the *Great Reform Act*, Blackburn's Vicar was John William Whittaker, who had married into the Feilden family, and whose resistance to Catholicism and Nonconformism was matched in its ferocity only by his contempt for reformism. He became the object of severe censure from the local branch of the Chartist movement (which campaigned for universal male suffrage), 4,000 of whose supporters occupied his church on 4 August 1839 to hear Whittaker preach to a text of their choosing, only to suffer a lengthy tirade in which they were described as 'malicious schemers' with only 'visionary fancies and revengeful passions'. His successor in the last decade of the century, Bishop Cramer-Roberts, told his congregation in a sermon on the loaves and fishes at one election that he 'hoped they would vote for the Conservative candidates, and thus support the Church'; and as late as 1910, Vicar Bishop Thornton appeared on a public platform with fifteen local clergy in support of the Conservatives.

The most notorious features of Victorian elections, however, were patronage and corruption, both between and within parties. With no secret ballot, candidates were able to offer inducements (ranging from hospitality to bonus payments to employees or even simple bribes) to Blackburn's 627 voters, and, if unsuccessful by generosity, used menace - as did the 98 per cent of Blackburnians who had no vote. Election campaigns were thus turbulent, murky affairs. Figures 3 to 6 are examples of contemporary election posters.

Disturbances at elections usually centred around Church Street: from 1832 onwards, the *Old Bull* in front of the Parish Church was the meeting-place of candidates' committees, and at that first election, John Bowring set up his campaign headquarters on the other side of Darwen Street in the home of radical poet Robert Clemesha. Bowring spoke from Clemesha's balcony, often inviting fierce debate with Tory opponents appearing from their headquarters at the windows of the *Old Bull*. William Turner was later accused of being 'the first to deluge the borough with drink' after he opened his campaign at the *Old Bull* by rolling beer-barrels into the churchyard for the inglorious satisfaction of his supporters, who supped amid the gravestones.

A procession of Bowring's supporters marched from the top of Montague Street to Bolton Road bearing banners and accompanied by a band. A crowd of 10,000 gathered to hear the nominations and

Figures 3-6. Victorian election posters, examples of the lively propaganda which plastered public walls in Blackburn at election time. *Blackburn Library*

ELECTORS

f BLACKBURN, of all Parties.

The Question is asked,
Why do not Candidates open **Bread** and **Cheese Shops** rather than Beer Shops ?
But the proper question to put to you Ten-Pounders , Why do you **require** or **expect** treating **any shape** ! **You** who hold the Elective Franchise **in trust** for your poorer fellow Subjects, **aid to be** less intelligent.
Do you take " a Gift which perverteth judgment" ?
f so, then the Radicals are quite right in demanding e extension of the Suffrage---in demanding that the ghts of Labour be represented, as well as the Interests of property." They are quite correct in serting that your (presumed) **intelligence,** is whit better than their (presumed) **ignorance,** y that so far from being **better,** it is as much **vorse** as the " sin against light and knowledge" is orse than the " sin of ignorance."
Electors reflect before you touch or taste the **MEAL** or **MALT** of any Candidate---you ay not be able to prevent that most disgraceful of all ecies of Bribery, the opening of Drink Shops---but ou may refuse to partake of it---*you may keep away om the degrading carousal,* and you may Refuse to artake of **ANY THING,** having the sem- ance of " *the gift*" designed " to pervert judgment."
A BROTHER ELECTOR.

MR. TURNER,

And his Committee *must* disclaim all connexions with a silly, though well-meant placard, signed " *a real Friend to the Poor*," who imputes to Mr. Turner many good deeds of which he himself never heard before. He cannot therefore take credit to himself for acts of charity which he never intended; for instance ;—

Before claiming *any* credit for benefactions to the Par- sonage, or Church, of Shrigley, valued so and so—he must admit that he purchased that Estate subject to the *condition* of *maintaining* these structures (which are his *own Pro- perty*) as much as Shrigley House, or Mill Hill.

While acknowledging that he has done *something* towards improving the Clergymans stipend at Shrigley, he cannot but express his deep regret that a report ever got abroad that a former Clergyman's Wife was obliged to fall on her very knees before the late Mrs. Turner, interceding for some little allow- ance for the *necessaries* of life.

Before alluding to his Subscriptions to other Churches, &c. Mr. Turner would rather wish it not to be mentioned how many of these Subscriptions are *yet unpaid.*

In looking forward to the new Era of *Free Trade,* now dawning upon us chiefly by his exertions, Mr. Turner's *be- nevolence* calls upon him to promise to his workmen at least *two days* work per week, with wages not *much* behind other houses, and *some* trifle for over-hours,——for the future.

Signed (by Order,)

JONADAB WOAD,

With consent of the Committee.

CHAIRMAN.

A SECOND MEMENTO
TO THE
ELECTORS
Of Blackburn.

I could wish to direct your particular attention to a placard just issued from Mr. Turner's press, calling on the "non-electors" and others both in and out of the Borough, "to *remember* that lists will be shortly published, shewing," in fact, whether or not you have voted in favour of Mr. Turner. The object of this clearly is to frighten you by a threat—if not of popular violence—yet at least of *non-intercourse* and *exclusive dealing*. If it mean not this, I call upon Mr. Turner and his Committee to say what *is* meant by this appeal to the electors and *non-electors* in and out of the Borough? It is nothing less, in spirit, than a clumsy, but sneaking imitation of an open and more honest attempt of the same kind, made by the Political Union in December 1832, in support of Bowring and in opposition to Mr Turner.

I hope then, Electors you *will* remember from what party this base attempt now proceeds:—It proceeds from the advocates of the Ballot! who now threaten to punish us, (if they can,) by means of publicity. It proceeds from that party who insulted and vilified Mr. Turner in 1832, on the hustings, and in their petitions, by means of Bowring and the *Gazette*,—as "*a hoary headed old sinner*," —as "*a promoter of beastly drunkenness*,"—as one who "*profaned the church-yard*" and even "*hoisted his filthy beer barrels on the tombs of our forefathers*." And yet these most virtuous purists,—these most consistent Apostles of *temperance* and *teetotalism* now not only support this same Mr. Turner, but have been as mute as fishes, while he, or his Committee have been again opening the "*flood-gates of intemperance*" in almost every beer-shop and pot house in the Borough.

Disapproving, strongly as I do of Mr. Turner's political conduct, I still personally respect him so much as to feel sorry to see him, wending his weary way through our streets, either alone, neither knowing nor known to,—those to whom he entirely owed his first election,—or else escorted by agents of that party which so lately bespattered him with every term of abuse, not sparing even his grey hairs. It is really pitiable to see him now trying to hobble into Parliament by the aid of Bowring's cast-off crutches.

This is the same party too, who after trying to *cheat* us *out of one half* of our franchise by dictating that we are *not* to split our votes, are now further trying to rob us of our freedom by an implied threat of exclusive dealing. But let us spurn with disdain such an impudent attempt to bully us, it is the mere whisper of an expiring faction, a decided proof of their weakness and despair,—a proof of their will, but not of their power to injure.

I have thrice voted for Mr. Turner, and to this present moment am free and unpledged. But I can now put no confidence in a man who deliberately belies his own vote of last year by voting that *he* has *now* confidence in a Ministry, which after unsettling every thing has settled nothing, and brought the nation to the verge of bankruptcy. The other two Candidates are as anxious and as deeply interested in *really* free trade and cheap every thing as he is. I will therefore *not* vote again for him, I will

Support Feilden and Hornby.

I remain,
Gentlemen, &c.

Blackburn, June 28th, 1841.   **CATO.**

WOOD, PRINTER, MARKET-PLACE, BLACKBURN.

LOCAL COLLECTION No. 4588

Whig-Radical
Alphabet

FOR THE USE OF OUR SCHOOL,

AT THE

New 10 Per Cent.

A's That *Old Cant* in Duke Street, whose *whine* is Cheap Bread.
B's A Fat Sappy Fellow called Swivel-eyed Ned.

C's a Sawney come South, who does nothing but scowl.
D's a *Screw* that's turned *Dipper*, a Doctor's the Owl.

E's a shocking bad lot that they call *Eccles' Cakes*.
F's a Riddled Necked Lawyer who their Dirty Work takes.

G's a *Drunken* Whig Doctor that rides a Grey Tit.
H's a White Livered Rad. *who should* teach the boys wit.

I's both for Peter and George, who conduct the Election.
J's a Big Bellied Green Grocer of *Tontine Perfection*.

K's a Black Muzzled *Tinker* they always call Mac.
L's a Silly Young Lawyer engaged as *a Hack*.

M's a Long Slinking Chartist who Governs a School.
N's David a Scotchman, by birthright a Fool.

O's a Letter which need not at present be seen.
P's the two *Razors* who 're so terribly keen.

Q's like the poor O, must be misunderstood.
R's that *Surly Scotch Jack* who does nobody good.

S'is an Ass of a Preacher, a Cooper, *a Skinner*.
T's an *Ex Member for Blackburn*, as I am a Sinner.

U's deserted, and therefore will make the list fewer.
V's a Man *with the Nose*, very like a *New brewer*.

W's the Mill Hill Pink, being both *Bully and Sot.*
X, Y, Z are disgusted and won't join such a lot.

P
05
1847

Vivat Turner et Vic.

315

results, and despite the recruitment of more special constables, the early closure of pubs and the prohibition of further parades, Bowring's unexpected 13-vote defeat caused riots in Ainsworth Street and around the *Old Bull* before Bowring himself appeared at Clemesha's window to appeal for calm.

A tradition of robust campaigning was thus established: in 1835, WH Hornby was thrown over Salford Bridge by a mob of Bowringites; in 1841 and 1853 his home in King Street was pelted with stones by a gang. Riots also broke out after William Turner's defeat in 1841 by one vote, whereupon a crowd of Turner's supporters which had met on Blakey Moor ransacked the Tory rooms at the *Bull*, gutting parts of the building and threatening patrons and staff. Only the appearance of the 61st Regiment restored order. As late as 1868, the hustings at The Wrangling were marred by a pitched battle between 50,000 supporters of rival candidates hurling discarded 'clinkers' at one another across feeble partitions.

In the second half of the century two victories - those of William Eccles in 1852 and of WH Hornby and Joseph Feilden in 1868 - were declared void after allegations of bribery and intimidation. In the latter, the Tories were held to have issued the threat (the 'screw circular') to sack workers in certain mills should they vote Liberal - and in some cases the threat was carried out. A few months later, the sacked workers marched to Preston to meet Prime Minister Gladstone, who, having heard their grievances, abandoned his opposition to the secret ballot, which he introduced in 1872. Back in Blackburn, however, the re-run of the election changed little, as the disgraced candidates were replaced by their sons.

Even the advent of the secret ballot did not end allegations of bullying, and as the Tories held Blackburn's seats with increasing security, tension grew within the dominant party. In 1875, the death of sitting MP HM Feilden occasioned a by-election in which three men sought the Conservative nomination. The matter was resolved at a turbulent meeting of 3,000 party supporters - workers and gentry - in the Exchange. The brewer, Daniel Thwaites, attracted considerable resentment because, though narrowly defeated as a Tory candidate in Blackburn the previous year, he had refused to commit himself to accepting the outcome of the meeting. The press were evicted from the meeting, and three votes had to be taken before it was declared that Thwaites had won. He went on to win the election, but only after the Liberals had endeavoured to persuade his chief rival, William Coddington, to stand as a 'Progressive Conservative', and despite allegations in the *Blackburn Times* that he had swayed the voters with his produce in the style of William Turner. The Liberal paper's editorial on 2 October 1875 ran:

> *'There are influences operating upon a large section of electors, of the lowest order in point of morality ... large numbers of men, presumably voters, had after the discharge of their electoral function, partaken with more freedom than discretion of exhilarating drinks. ... Whether it was paid for by the drinkers themselves, or won in the nature of a bonus for*

adherence to constitutional principles in the trying hour, or was a small foretaste of the splendid legacy Mr. Thwaites means to give to every inhabitant of Blackburn in his last will, it appeared all the same an extravagance. ... If Mr. Daniel Thwaites sold all the beer that was drunk on and off the premises this week in connection with the election, what a pretty penny he must have turned by the contest!'

Wealth and influence continued to be important aspects of politics in Blackburn even after the electorate grew to 15 per cent of the town's population in 1885, because voters were encouraged to stay loyal to candidates who provided not only a wage packet and a roof over their heads, but also contributed to a multitude of local activities. In 1900, their last fully successful appeal to Blackburn's voters, Tories WH Hornby and William Coddington boasted that they were 'men who have known you all their lifetime, and have contributed to almost everything in the town, from the boys' football and cricket clubs to bazaars of all denominations'. In all, they claimed to have supported as many as 900 local organisations.

The dynamics of Victorian elections were more varied than the images of blatant bribery and mob violence suggest. For at least some of the time, the interests of employers and townspeople coincided, as for example over free trade. This sense of town pride, reflected on occasions such as the reception given to Blackburn Olympic FC by the town's MPs upon their FA Cup victory in 1883, and the local MPs' support thereafter for Rovers. The townspeople repaid this contact with symbolic gifts awarded at mass meetings of operatives, and with repeated office in Parliament and the council for their masters. This relationship, if nothing else, was relatively successful in integrating a rapidly-expanding population into the political process. Militant movements - whether Chartism in the 1840s, the Reform League in the 1860s, or the Suffragettes after 1900 - found curiously little enthusiasm in Blackburn. Engels complained to Marx of the 1868 election in Blackburn that 'once again, the proletariat has discredited itself terribly'. Certainly, the town had its disturbances, but many of these were caused by the results of elections as much as the absence of democracy, and none was as sustained or serious as the conflicts which consumed other parts of the country from time to time. Blackburn's people had withstood the worst the industrial revolution had to offer, and had believed that they could control events through constitutional politics. That hope was to be both fulfilled and further tested in the twentieth century.

1900-55: The Rise of Labour

The first half of the twentieth century saw two new developments displace old guiding forces of Blackburn's affairs. As the authority of churches and dominant employers waned, other factors came to have a determining influence in the age of universal suffrage.

Firstly, the tradition of local men representing Blackburn came to an end. Of those elected for the first time for Blackburn since 1900, only one, John Duckworth, Liberal MP from 1923-29, fits the model of the local cotton manufacturer. The remainder include a civil servant from Cowling in Yorkshire; an international lawyer from Dunfermline, a Manchester merchant, a trade unionist from Driffield, and a Surrey-based writer from Leicester. This change reflects both a national trend away from local interests, but also the inability of a town in decline to supply local dignitaries prepared to invest their time in a declining Parliament. As present MP Jack Straw commented in a recent interview, '*Blackburn's voters treat their MPs like their footballers - they don't care where they come from, as long as they get the best for Blackburn*'.

Secondly, and likewise reflecting national events, this was a period of transition for the parties, with a greater turnover of MPs. The country experienced 21 years of coalition government, and witnessed the replacement of the Liberals by the Labour Party. In Blackburn, this latter trend was particularly pronounced, since where the Liberals had weakened to the point of not offering candidates in Blackburn by 1900, the town's industrial, working-class character made it promising ground for Labour.

The earliest evidence of this came in 1900 when Philip Snowden (Figure 7), the radical stump orator of the still embryonic Labour Party, won a larger vote than any other Labour candidate. The size of this poll caused William Coddington to retire from the contest in 1906, when Snowden was elected as Blackburn's first Labour MP. Although at times locked out by arrangements between Liberal and Conservative organisations, Labour won both Blackburn seats in 1929, when

Figure 7. Cigarette card of Philip Snowden, a leading figure in the early Labour Party, who represented Blackburn for twelve years before becoming Chancellor of the Exchequer. *Author.*

MR. PHILIP SNOWDEN.

Liberal representation came to an end, and again in 1945. Between 1912 and 1930, the number of workers and trade unionists on Blackburn council trebled.

As many continuities as changes are observable in developments during this period, however Blackburn's voters remained cautious, and committed to certain key principles such as patriotism. Thus in 1918 they evicted Philip Snowden for his doubts about the conduct of the Great War (despite, or perhaps because of, the appearance of war poet Siegfried Sassoon in his support). Likewise, the penchant for characters remained, except that now they became national rather than local celebrities: Snowden was a leading figure in the Labour Party, and eventually became its first Chancellor of the Exchequer; his successor as Labour MP Mary Agnes Hamilton wrote six biographies, numerous novels, and was a member of the Balfour Commission on Trade and Industry as well as later a governor of the BBC. Before the Second World War Barbara Castle's (Figure 8) fire-

Figure 8. Barbara Castle in her early electioneering days. She was the town's MP for many years and a much loved figure. *Blackburn Library*

brand speeches gained national news coverage and helped secure her nomination from a local Labour Party uneasy about female candidates. She went on to become that rare commodity - a Cabinet minister widely remembered with affection. For the Conservatives, Ralph Assheton, the last Conservative member for Blackburn, came from a family which had owned land in Lancashire since Elizabethan times, and whose ancestors had been called to Parliament as early as 1382. He had already been national Chairman of the Conservative Party, held various junior government posts, and become a renowned pioneer of free-market ideas, before he won Blackburn West in 1950.

Lastly, Blackburn's public continued to participate in the pageant of politics when occasion arose: Philip Snowden, who had held regular mass meetings in the market square since the end of the nineteenth century, was welcomed in 1910 at the station by a victory parade of 500 torchbearers taking him to a 'monster gathering' of well-wishers. Snowden's first election victory, indeed, was achieved on an impressive 95 per cent turnout. Blackburn also welcomed the Prime Minister for the first time when Chamberlain addressed a mass meeting in King George's Hall in March 1939, at the height of the pre-war crisis.

1955-97: Redevelopment, Race and Recession

Since 1955, Blackburn has had only one seat, held throughout by Labour. The Conservative share of the vote at Parliamentary elections has declined from 49.5 per cent in 1955 to under a quarter in 1997 - the party's lowest ever in Blackburn. Local pride and caution have, however, remained the watchwords of the voters

Local pride was best illustrated by the programme of town centre redevelopment steered through by George Eddie and Robert Mottershead for the two main parties on the council, and finally completed in 1979. Here and in the more recent City Challenge, politicians of different parties have united for the good of the town.

Caution, on the other hand, can be seen in the treatment by the townspeople of the sensitive issue of race. The growth of the ethnic minority population of Blackburn from under 1,000 in 1960 to over 20,000 in the 1990s raised tensions and dilemmas for all concerned, and threatened at times to become an explosive issue. During the 1970s, the far-Right saw Blackburn as one of its most promising areas: Enoch Powell was the guest of honour at a local Conservative Association fete in 1969, and at this and a series of other meetings in the town centre, demonstrations by the National Front and counter-demonstrations from their opponents disrupted the routine of Blackburn life. Blackburn was indeed the focus of a vigorous recruitment campaign by the NF, and in 1975 earned national notoriety as the first town to elect two councillors for the breakaway far-Right National Party of John Kingsley Read.

Commentary by visiting journalists and some of the local press exaggerated the deterioration of community relations, and some coverage presented Blackburn in an unreasonably poor light. The fact is that no party profited seriously from attempts to stir up hostility to immigrants: the demonstrations, though highly visible, involved no more than a few thousand protesters, mostly from outside the town, and came to an end after 1978. The National Front never gained more than a derisory 4.4 per cent of Blackburn's parliamentary poll, and the NP was unable to capitalise upon its fleeting success (one of the two councillors resigned almost immediately, and the other was ousted at the next election). Throughout, Blackburn returned MPs from the party most committed to Race Relations legislation, and most hostile to the demands of the far-Right. Race was and remains a delicate issue - but by and large, the scepticism of Blackburn voters kept them away from simplistic solutions, and kept their most urgent thoughts elsewhere.

The most pressing issue in post-war Blackburn has been economic decline, and it is in part this that has consolidated Labour's position. In 1983, when Labour suffered its worst national performance since the 1930s, and changes in the boundaries of the constituency drew in Tory-dominated districts beyond Billinge, Jack Straw maintained a healthy majority partly because of local resentment at 18 per cent unemployment (the 87th highest figure of 650 constituencies in Britain).

The tradition of backing MPs who maintained local contact with flair persisted, too. Barbara Castle and Jack Straw continued the practice of regular town-centre open-air meetings, the former even bringing Frankie Vaughan to sing to shoppers during an election campaign. Castle helped out in floods by rowing to victims' houses, and Straw makes the news by personally catching criminals in the street near his surgery. Both have brought their Prime Ministers to the town, and Straw has drawn national attention in the 1990s in connection with everything from the first multi-million pound lottery win to Rovers winning the Premiership. These are the characteristics Blackburn likes - and having decided it likes an MP, it is reluctant to switch.

Conclusion

Recent accounts claim Blackburn exhibits the same 'antipathy to political extremism' and 'tendency towards political conservatism' described in the columns of the *Northern Daily Telegraph* back in 1900; less charitably, this has been interpreted as evidence of 'public apathy'. However, as any student of political affairs will confirm, being radical and militant are not the only ways of being political and exercising power. Blackburn's power was harnessed, for the good of the town and the country at large, by its voters and leaders, in times of change and hardship. Rather than berating the town, it might be fairer to salute the stability and unity of purpose, the prudent caution and scepticism of Blackburn's public and politicians. Perhaps the best man to do that is one native to the town, and who, despite coming bottom of the poll in 1869 in what he remembered as a 'forlorn' bid, went on to become a statesman and man of letters of the early twentieth century; a Cabinet minister for twelve years and Chancellor of Manchester University, who took the name of his home town when made a Viscount in 1908. His tribute to Blackburn says much about its people and its politics:

> '*In a Lancashire valley at the foot of bleak, stern, moorland ridges lies what is now the important and prosperous manufacturing town of Blackburn ... The people had a character with marked force of its own. Ready to respect where respect on any good ground was due, they are ready, too with a blunt pride that is no bad form of self-respect. They have always had the virtues of fraternal and genial plain speakers; they show themselves independent, shrewd, quick, keen-bitten. They have a cherished vernacular with broad accent and original vocabulary, which enables them to do apt justice to any of their opinions and emotions*'

John Morley (1838-1923), 1st Viscount Morley of Blackburn,
Recollections, Vol. 1 (1917).

7. The Blue Plaque Trail of Darwen

by Jan Gill and Mary Whittaker

OUR BLUE PLAQUE TRAIL WILL TAKE YOU from one end of Darwen to the other end. You will learn something about the industry with which the town is usually associated, but don't let this deceive you into thinking that this is all that there is to the town, which was old long before the Industrial Revolution, and which has a character that owes at least as much to nature as to industry; it also has a beauty of its own that man hasn't yet completely destroyed.

Our Blue Plaque Trail starts at the southern boundary of the town - the boundary with Bolton. There is a walk of a mile or so from here to the first Blue Plaque; a walk that takes you over Bull Hill, which is steeper than you think, but which helps you to see the glorious views. To the west, on your left, is a panorama of hills, sky and cattle, with Darwen Tower coming into view, looking like a space rocket about to take off. To the east there are more rolling hills and moors, dwellings, farm buildings, trees, and, in the distance, Blacksnape Ridge, a route familiar to the Romans as they travelled from Manchester to Ribchester. At any time of the year this view is spectacular; in the delicate colours of Spring, and the glorious tones of autumn, it is really magnificent.

Bull Hill was recorded on the map of 1786 published by William Yates, a customs officer and surveyor from Liverpool. There were few dwellings in this area in the eighteenth century - there are not so many here today, despite the new development at Woodlea Chase, the new residential area on the site of Bull Hill Hospital. You need to be hardy, like the local farmers, to cope with the cold, wind-swept moors at this altitude. In the eighteenth century handloom weaving was the main industry, along with coal mining and quarrying. By the mid-nineteenth century, approximately one third of the population was employed in the manufacturing of textiles, but by this time there were more power loom weavers than handloom weavers. Other occupations in the mid-eighteenth century included coal mining, quarry work, joinery, stone mason's work, transport, and domestic work.

An Act of Parliament passed in 1797 stated that the road between Bolton and Blackburn was hilly in parts, narrow, awkward and much

Figure 1. Mural on gable end by tram reversing triangle. *Mary Whittaker*

in need of repair. This road follows a route which is similar to the present A666, at least between Blackburn and Darwen, and we follow it from Bull Hill to Whitehall, which is also recorded on William Yates' map. There is also a coal mine recorded on the map, at Cranberry Moss, which is about one quarter of a mile from the road to Bolton; there were coalmines at Whitehall in the early

Figure 2. Blue plaque at reversing triangle. *Mary Whittaker.*

nineteenth century; details of these, along with mines at Earnsdale, and Hoddlesden are referred to in a contemporary newspaper, the *Blackburn Mail*. It is uncertain how long these mines were worked; a map of 1847 shows quite a few old coal pits, so they might not have been worked for long. Coal mining was widespread throughout Darwen.

The houses and shops that we pass en route are much newer than those of the 1786 map; our first Blue Plaque is at the Tramway Reversing Triangle (Figures 1 and 2), opened on 5 December 1881; it was the southern terminus of the first steam powered street tramway in the United Kingdom. Blackburn and Over Darwen Tramway was opened on 14 April 1881 (Figure 3). The Blackburn

Figure 3. Steam tram. *Darwen Library*

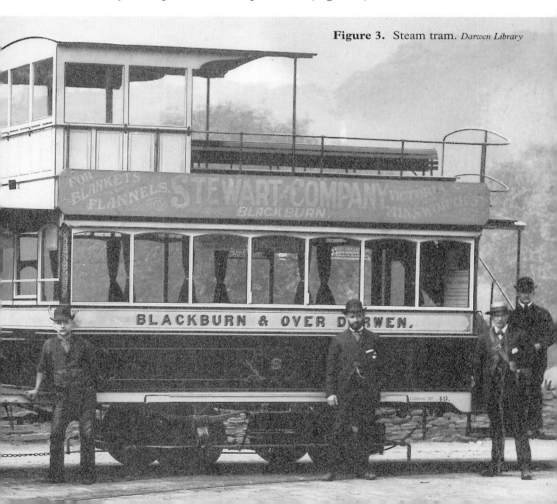

and Over Darwen Tramways Company was formed in 1880 to enable a steam operated line to be built, to run from St Peter's Street in Blackburn, to Darwen. Passenger services began the following year. In 1898 the undertaking was bought, jointly, by Blackburn and Darwen Corporations. Blackburn Corporation Tramways Company was the second private firm to be registered, and this was in 1886; this Company was to operate routes within the Borough of Blackburn. In February, 1900, work began on the electrification of the tramway between Blackburn and Darwen. A branch line to Hoddlesden was opened in 1901. Trams were succesful for a number of years, ultimately they could not compete with the manoeuverability and versatility of buses, and, despite a reprieve caused by petrol shortages in the Second World War, the tram era came to an end in 1949.

From the Tramway Reversing Triangle, we walk along the main road until we come to Buryfold Lane, and Low Hill House, which was built in 1812. For about five years, from 1817 it was the home of Samuel Crompton and his two sons. Samuel Crompton invented the Spinning Mule in 1779; this was a combination of the ideas of Arkwright and Hargreaves. The Spinning Mule was adopted widely, but Crompton, who was a sensitive person, and a poor businessman, gained little financial reward from it.

Crompton was born in 1752, in Bolton; his family was involved in textiles, and farming. Shortly after Samuel's birth the family fortunes, in decline for some time, declined still further, and the family had to move, first to a small cottage, then to Hall i' th' Wood. Mr Crompton died when Samuel was five years old; his mother taught him how to spin and to weave. The spinning jenny he used frequently broke down, and the delays necessitated by constantly mending it incurred his mother's wrath. He had a lonely, hardworking childhood, with one consolation - music; an early indication of Samuel's mechanical talents was when he made a fiddle. He spent five years, from 1774 to 1779, thinking about, and planning the spinning machine he was to invent, which would improve the yarn he was able to spin, then weave on his own loom. He had few tools, and, as he earned little from his spinning and weaving, he supplemented his income by playing in an orchestra in the theatre at Bolton. He had to teach himself to use the new tools he bought, as he wanted to keep his invention a secret, although it eventually became known that he was building some sort of machine. Its completion coincided with the destruction of machines by workers fearing for the loss of their jobs and Crompton's Spinning

Mule became a target. Fortunately, he took precautions against this, and his invention survived. He married shortly after this, to the daughter of Mr Pimott, a West Indian merchant. The marriage was a happy one, and the couple had sons, but Samuel suffered through his lack of business acumen, and because others took advantage of his honesty.

Low Hill House was later occupied by Eccles Shorrock, who added the east and west wings of the house. Eccles Shorrock was a well-known business man in Darwen and was responsible for building India Mill and its unique chimney.

From Low Hill House we continue along Bolton Road to India Mill, to the wallpaper surface printing machine which stands at the roadside in front of it. This machine was donated by Crown Wallcoverings Ltd. This type of machine was used in Darwen from the middle of the 19th century, and it was instrumental in establishing a world reputation for British wallpapers. It is fitted with twelve printing stations, each capable of printing a different colour, seven print rollers are in position.

Crown wallcoverings occupies a site at Belgrave, at the bottom of Bolton Road, where the Belgrave Works was situated. It was begun in 1836, and was one of the largest paper-staining works in the country; over 250 people were employed here. Almost half of these were children. In 1838, Charles and Harold Potter and Walmsley Preston, a foreman at Potter's works, adapted the surface calico printing machine to produce wallpaper. (Preston had initiated many of the experiments relating to the new technique to be carried out). By 1840, the Potters were manufacturing wallpaper at Belgrave. There were extensions to the building in 1880, and in 1899 Wallpaper Manufacturers Ltd was established here. This was acquired by the Reed Group in 1964, and in 1970 the Crown Products group was formed. Although the company has changed hands yet again, the building, seen from the main road, still bears the legend *Crown Wallcoverings*.

Close to the wallpaper surface printing machine is an engine used in the textile trade, although this does not actually have a blue plaque. It is a cross compound horizontal mill engine, which formerly powered one of the weaving sheds at India Mill.

We continue along Bolton Road, then up Church Street, to the Blue Plaque on the wall of Hanbury's Supermarket. This building, almost in the shadow of St Peter's, the Parish Church of Darwen, was the site of the Peel Baths, erected by public subscription in 1853. From 1854-1878 the Local Board of Health Offices were located here, and from 1871-1895 the first library was here. The Borough of Darwen Corporation Offices were here from 1878-1882. The Baths were closed in 1933, and were demolished in 1963.

In 1854, when there were about 11,000 people in the town, the Local Board was formed; this administered the affairs of the town for twenty-five years. By the end of that period, there were about 22,000 people in Darwen, and it was felt that the town could cope with having a mayor and a corporation. A meeting of ratepayers was held in the Co-operative Hall; a resolution was passed on 20 May, 1877, in favour of incorporation. The following November the Privy Council granted a charter of incorporation. On 25 March, 1878, the document was conveyed to the town by Mr Snape, who was chairman of the Local Board; the bells of Holy Trinity, the Parish Church, now known as St Peter's, pealed. On 1 July, 1878, the first Town Council was elected, with Mr Snape as Mayor, an office he held for three years.

It was reported by Dr Armitage, the Medical Officer, on 31 August 1889, that the health of the Borough continued to be good; 56 male babies were born, and 45 female.

We walk back down Church Street, on to the main road, which now becomes Market Street. There is a plaque on the wall between the Abbey National Building Society and the Argos shop; this was the site of the Market House and Assembly Rooms, erected by Eccles Shorrock in 1847. The first floor also housed the Mechanics Institute, and first magistrates court. In 1882 the building was converted to shops; part of the building was demolished in 1990.

By 1847, it was common in the Lancashire towns, and in most of the villages, for educational organisations to have been founded which catered for the needs of the working people. Some of these organisations, like the mechanics' institutes, received a lot of help from the employers; in some, the members paid for everything out of their subscriptions. Education for the masses was not widely advocated, or accepted, when the first of the mechanics' institutes was founded. The movement was promoted by Lord Brougham, who was initially in the minority when he stated that 'liberality and enlightened toleration' needed knowledge; he was proved to be correct, however, and, later, more and more support was given by the upper and middle classes. The first institute in Lancashire was formed in Manchester in 1824. When the institutes began, the students often had to be taught the Three R's before they could be taught the scientific instruction which the innovators of the movement were so keen on.

From here we walk along to School Street, then walk up it to the plaque on Netto (Figure 4), part of a new block of shops which was built in 1993; the foundation stone for the new shop was laid by Eileen Entwistle, who was, at that time, Mayor of Blackburn. The Blue Plaque on the side of Netto marks the site of the Darwen Industrial Co-operative Society Ltd (whose buildings ran the length of School Street, Figure 5). The foundation stones were laid by Thomas Hughes, QC, author of *Tom Brown's Schooldays*, on 29 December 1866 and 8 December 1894. An office block was built in 1911-12; this was demolished in 1989.

Co-operative movements are formed when people join together to pool their resources

Figure 4. Blue plaque at site of Industrial Co-operative Society's central stores. *Mary Whittaker*

Figure 5. Industrial Co-operative Society's central stores. *Darwen Library*.

for joint economic growth; this help can be in the form of manufacturing, or giving credit. Under the influence of Robert Owen, the first principles of the co-operative movement began in Rochdale in 1844, and came to Darwen in 1860. Robert Owen was a socialist; amongst other things, he created a model village in New Lanark in Scotland, at the beginning of the nineteenth century.

From here, we continue up School Street, to Knott Street, then to Railway Road, to the Blue Plaque which commemorates the Blackburn to Bolton Railway (Figure 6). The first sod of the Blackburn to Bolton Railway was cut by the Chairman, W H Hornby, close to Over Darwen Station, on 27 September, 1845. The line was opened between Blackburn and Sough on the 3 August 1847, and between Sough and Bolton on 12 June, 1848. Objections from the East Lancashire Railway meant that the Blackburn, Darwen and Bolton Railway had to run their trains over the East Lancashire Railway line between Bolton Road and Daisyfield; this led to a dispute over tolls, and there was a blockade by the East Lancashire Railway on the day of opening. In 1856 the Blackburn, Darwen and Bolton Company was taken over by the East Lancashire and Lancashire and Yorkshire Railways. In 1962, passenger operations on the above line ceased; the route is still used for diversions, goods

Figure 6. Darwen station. *Darwen Library*

traffic and special excursions; the route to Bolton is still fully used, and remains Blackburn's only rail link with Manchester.

From here, we walk down Railway Road, to Knott Street, down Union Street past the Police Station, the Health Centre and the Fire Station and the Social Services offices, to Market Street. We continue along the main road, which becomes Duckworth Street, then Blackburn Road, and walk for about a mile until we reach 'Nellie', which is on the roadside just before Darwen Vale High School. Nellie is a vertical steam engine which was built by George Ruston of Lodge Bank Darwen, at Sunnybank Mill, in April 1898. It was last operated in December 1972. The weight of the fly wheel is 3.5 tons. The Machine was preserved in March 1978. Sunnybank Mill, a paper staining works, was built by John and James Brandwood, c1855. There was accommodation for ninety looms in the buildings. It was leased to Stafford, Standing and Duckworth. The mill was taken over by Potters in 1858, then closed down. After 1858, a variety of cloth manufacturers used the buildings, including James Garstang, J & J Aspen and J & J Gregson. The mill was converted to hard waste spinning in 1867 by James Watson. A single storey building, which has a brick façade, still stands, on the site of the cotton mill.

We then continue to the northern boundary at Craven's Brow, just a few hundred yards from 'Nellie', which is the final point, for now, of our Blue Plaque Trail.

8. VERY PROPER: CHARLES TIPLADY AND HIS DIARY 1829 - 1873

by Jim Heyes

MR TIPLADY CLOSES THE SHUTTERS of his shop in Church Street at the end of a working day. This is a special day, his sixtieth birthday in fact. His workmen and apprentices have gone home to their evening meal. There is time for him to reflect at the end of a busy day before he, too, must make his own way home.

June has been exceptionally fine, bringing warm, balmy days, transforming the delight of spring into early summer. Four days before, on the Sunday, the pattern had broken with cloudbursts and thunderstorms, bringing welcome rain for the gardens.

A week earlier, Charles Tiplady had attended the Grand Masonic Festival in Lancaster, one of the 1500 brother Freemasons marching in procession to witness the laying of the foundation stone of the Royal Albert Asylum.

All in all, a memorable time, Tiplady writes in his diary:

> *My sixtieth birthday. Truly the shadows of evening are falling fast around me. Thanks be to God for his sparing mercies. Birthday gifts from my children, etc.*

The Diary

Most of us have kept a diary, a pocket type perhaps, or a desk diary for appointments. Often they serve only as a reminder to visit the dentist or buy a birthday card, rarely are they kept as they once were, as personal and intimate records of private thought and feeling. Published diaries can bring fame, as did Samuel Pepy's diary, and politicians often keep a diary with a view to future publication.

Lancashire has its share of historic diaries, a rich source of information. Ellen Weeton's Journal chronicles the life of a governess in South West Lancashire, and the diary of James Ward, a cotton spinner near Clitheroe in the 1860s, is a major document of social history.

Charles Tiplady worked as a printer and bookseller in Blackburn for 40 years. His father's family had originated in Morton near Bingley in the West Riding of Yorkshire. Tiplady's diary tells us that one Richard Tiplady, who died there in the 1840's, had been a well-to-do farmer, whose property was eventually contested for, and won, by Charles's father, Thomas Tiplady. This Richard Tiplady was namesake to a great-uncle of the Blackburn branch of the family.

Tiplady's father remains a shadowy figure, barely mentioned in the diary, but Charles was evidently close to his brother William, and took him into his business. Charles Tiplady was born in Blackburn on 23 June 1808, the fourth child of Thomas Tiplady and his wife Elizabeth. There were eight children in all, four sons and four daughters. Elizabeth had been the oldest of the two daughters of James Lomax, whose family was long established in Blackburn. (Figure 1). The Tipladys cherished the Lomax name so much that many of the children had it as a second Christian name.

Rogerson's Directory of 1818 lists Thomas Tiplady as a 'traveller',

Figure 1. Blackburn in 1824 by James Gillies, showing a town hardly altered from the previous century. The Leeds and Liverpool Canal crosses the bottom of the plan, a vital artery transporting coal, raw cotton and building materials. Montague Street is no more than an intended line of road and open fields cluster close to the heart of the town. *Blackburn Library.*

but no trade or manufacture is indicated. The family lived at St John's, and the young Charles was educated at the National School in Thunder Alley. The diary occasionally mentions his school companions, and often with some affection. His education must have been adequate enough to prepare him for work as a printer. He served an apprenticeship with Thomas Rogerson who had a printing business in the old market place.

The Tipladys worshipped at the parish church of St John's, where Charles was a sidesman and churchwarden in later life, as well as being a Sunday School teacher at Grimshaw Park and Thunder Alley School. He leaves little information about his early life, though a letter written in June 1849, when he compared the River Blakewater of the 1840's with the stream he remembers some thirty years earlier gives some insight:

> *Then how beautiful to stroll by the devious courses, along the fields to Brookhouse, to the rookery at Little Harwood Hall; and on to the confines of the Sour Milk Farm. Then following this lazy current, we came to Whitebirk. There we sat down on its banks, listening to the sweet carolling of the birds, ever and anon refreshing ourselves with copious draughts of the pure liquid, and, pulling our homely crust of pie from our pockets, feasted right merrily. Ah, those were happy days, but now, poor old brook, how art thou fallen.*

By the 1840s, the Blakewater had become a polluted industrial sewer, unhealthy and dangerous. Tiplady believed his letter prompted the Improvement Commission to put work in hand to clear the brook, temporarily improving the flow of water.

In 1834, Charles married Miss Mary Heaton. There were two children from the marriage: Maria-Anne, born in 1835, who died two years later, and Thomas, who was said to be living in Liverpool in the 1890s. Mary died while still young, and was buried at St John's.

Charles remarried in 1839 to Miss Mary Callis at St Mary's, the parish church. His new wife was the daughter of grocer William Callis, whose shop at Salford lay close to Tiplady's shop in Church Street. Charles and Mary had seven children, five sons and two daughters.

The diary's records of his family often reveal his affections for them. He seems to have been a devoted family man. He was deeply affected by the death of his mother, and of his brother, elated at the birth of his son, and cast into despair at the death of his infant daughter. Mary Callis was disabled by a stroke in February 1868, and Charles' own health was often poor. An unspecified event in

February 1828 had almost caused his death at the age of twenty, but a greater trial came later.

Diary 14 April 1864

I underwent the operation for the stone; was reduced to the point of death, and did not recover from the effect until the month of August. About the 7th of June I went with Mrs Tiplady to Lytham, where I sojourned seven weeks.

The bracing air of Lytham revived Charles, but the diary has fewer entries for this period than for other years. Later, he recorded the passing of the Emperor Napoleon III, and commented that they had each undergone the same operation, Tiplady having fared better. The diary shows how each birthday prompted him to take stock of his life:

Diary 23 June 1860

52 years old this day. In health. Thank God for a life of mercies!

Diary 23 June 1870

My 62nd birthday. Weather brilliant; health good.

After his return home from convalescence he records that the family had a new home; 2, St Alban's Place, Blackburn, bought for the princely sum of £300, close to their former home. Soon afterwards, Charles's son Richard returned from Bahia after an absence of six years.

Charles was known for his skill at composing verse, usually for special events. None appear in dialect, however, as did the work of many of his contemporaries. There were many occasions to celebrate as Blackburn prospered.

Diary 28 January 1848

This day witnessed the imposing, and to Blackburn, important ceremony of opening the Market House, erected by the Commissioners under the Improvement Act. The structure is neat, handsome and spacious. There was a procession, followed by a public dinner. The event was the occasion of my composing lines 'On the Opening of the Market House, Blackburn' which were received with approbation.

It was indeed a red letter day for the town, celebrating the removal of the market to a new site, its home for the next 100 years. Redevelopment in the 1960s swept it away along with the rest of the town's rich Victorian heritage. Nothing that was lost in that turbulent decade caused as much public anguish and dismay as the loss of the much loved market landmark.

Weekly markets had been held in Blackburn from the sixteenth century, at least, and by the early years of the last century, the market cross, standing at the junction of Church Street and Darwen Street, was the focus for weekly markets, occasional fairs and regular cattle markets. The latter were moved to Blakey Moor in the years 1819-1820, whilst just five years later, *Baines's Directory* had the comment:

> *The want of a good market is much felt in Blackburn.*

Although Blackburn in the 1820s was still relatively undeveloped it was clear that markets in the main streets impeded traffic. No remedy was available until the *1847 Improvement Act*, which enabled the Commissioners to acquire a site in Sudell's Croft for a covered Market Hall. Architect Terence Flanagan designed a structure with

Figure 2. Blackburn market with its distinctive frontage had opened for business on 28 January 1848. This inspired one of Tiplady's verses, a paen to civic pride. *Author.*

an iron framework, large enough for three roof spans, and featuring a clock tower after the style of an Italian campanile, the whole costing £9,000. A separate fish market was added in 1868. The structure was to last through Victoria's reign and two world wars. (Figure 2). The community sense of achievement was expressed in Tiplady's verse:

Loud ring the merry peal with gladsome sound!
O'er every native hill the shout rebound.
Be this a day of honour to the Town!
Worthy to Children's Children handed down!
Be hushed the stern approach, the bitter sneer;
Let scornful finger not be pointed here.
BLACKBURN beside her neighbour towns shall stand
To boast a worthy name within our land;
Her commerce flourish, and her wealth increase.

Charles Tiplady's diary no longer exists in its original form. The manuscript text made by him was still extant during the 1880s when it was edited, transcribed and published in the local press by William Alexander Abram (1835-1894), Blackburn's first historian and antiquarian, librarian of the free library, editor of the *Blackburn Times* and long-serving town councillor. Abram edited the diary with typical Victorian regard for the sanctity of the private material contained within it, and in his preamble remarks:

Of course there is much in the Diary which is of too private a nature for publication. All such parts I have scrupulously omitted, but there is no harm in including, as has been done, entries which relate to the external activities of the Diarist himself.

With only few exceptions, Tiplady's inner thoughts and feelings have been clinically removed, leaving the diary as a rich source of local history, but with only a sketchy portrait of its author.

Many themes recur throughout the pages of diary, among them Tiplady's love of travel.

Diary 25 May 1841

J Forrest called and requested me to go to Blackpool with him in his Gin. I did so, partly expecting that this mode of travel would be cheaper, but I found that the day's expenses were £1 3s 6d, viz

	£	s	d
Bars to Preston		1	4
Horse do do and Gin		2	0

Tea at Lytham	2	3
Bars to do		6
Breakfast and Tea at Blackpool	4	6
Horse at Blackpool	3	6
Expense to Fleetwood	1	7
Shrimps for home	1	3
Bars home	1	10
Horse at Preston, etc	2	0
Breakfast at Lytham	2	3
Horse and Ostler do	0	6
1	3s	6d

The 'bars' itemised here were the turnpike tolls which travellers had to pass between towns. The journey, though 'fine and agreeable', worried Charles on account of its cost. He calculated separately cost for coach and rail travel, and concluded that a train journey from Preston to Blackpool would have cost him six shillings!

In 1853, Tiplady and his wife went on a tour.

Diary 27 September to 5 October 1853

Took a tour with Mrs Tiplady; our first since our marriage in 1839. Blackpool, Lytham, Fleetwood, Isle of Man.

Three years later, the couple enjoyed a day's excursions to Whittle Springs, a popular local venue. It was a hot August day. The hotel and pleasure gardens there were fashionable with day-trippers on the canal from Blackburn, East Lancashire and Wigan, many of whom sampled the renowned medicinal spring waters.

December 1859 brought hard frosts, cold, biting winds and a heavy fall of snow, but, after Boxing Day, the weather turned milder.

Diary 28 December 1859

Thawing. Went to Darwen, thence to Tockholes round the hillside, up to Sandford and Haydock's Mill. Met them and their workpeople at the Victoria Inn; a large party and a very happy meeting, plenty of good singing. Perhaps as clean, neat and pretty a set of factory hands as ever sat down at a feast.

Charles travelled to Newton-le-Willows in August 1860 to see the review of the Lancashire volunteers. Most Lancashire towns were represented in the volunteer corps formed in 1839.

On a trip to Liverpool in 1861 he saw one of the wonders of the world.

Diary 14 June 1861

The 'Great Eastern' at Liverpool; visited the great ship with Mrs Tiplady and daughter Fanny.

The Seasons

Two themes are paramount in the diary: the deaths of family, friends and fellow townsmen; and the weather. He confirms our nostalgic perceptions of springs and summers gone by.

Diary 30 April 1842.

The weather during the whole of the month has been exceedingly dry and sunny, with an east, north east and south east wind. In Blackburn, with the exception of the 24th, no rain fell.

Diary 13 June 1842

The weather since the commencement of June has been oppressively hot, the thermometer frequently rising upwards of 100 degrees . . . . This morning. . . we had a shower of rain, which would be found very beneficial.

Ten years later, the spring months were also exceptionally dry:

Diary 28 April 1852

After excessive drought of 70 days the wind changed from east to south and west, and we had rain today. It is said that there were more vessels waiting outside the channel (mouth of the Mersey) for change of wind than ever was known before.

Diary 30 June 1861

The month of June is ended; perhaps in the memory of the oldest inhabitants there has been no finer weather.

But even these halcyon days were overshadowed by the summer of 1868.

Diary 27 July 1868

Excessively hot. The 21st was considered the hottest day ever known in England. Thermometer, 101 in the shade, 123 in the sun. No rain; all dried up and parched. Cholera cases prevalent.

Diary 6 - 7 August 1868

The drought ended with fine showers of rain, and in some places thunder.

If some of these long ago summers were wonderfully hot, the winters in mid-Victorian Lancashire could be at the extreme of cold.

Diary 16 November 1861

First fall of snow this Winter - heavy, followed by a keen frost - Times fairly gloomy; work scarce: cotton dear; money bad to get; yet the population seem healthy.

Sometimes the winter weather produced a bonus when the frost was so severe that the reservoir at Rishton froze over. It became a mecca for skaters.

Diary 24 January 1858

About this time a very severe frost commenced and continued without intermission until the 20 February. All the great rivers in the kingdom - Thames, Severn, Mersey, Exe, Dee, Ribble, etc - were frozen over.

Diary 18 February 1855 - Sunday

A sort of Fair was held on Rishton Reservoir; from 8,000 to 10,000 people visited it; the ice was over two feet thick.

The inherent danger of skating on a frozen reservoir did not diminish its popularity, but on January 1870 Tiplady reported that four young people were drowned when the ice gave way. One, Hannah Towers, had promised her mother she wouldn't go on the ice, but had given in to a friend's urging. Severe storms featured in the diary, notably the great storm of 1839.

Diary 7 January 1839.

The great storm of wind when the Church was unroofed on the 7th of January 1839. Many chimneys were also blown down.

George C Miller in *Bygone Blackburn* related that the storm was in fact a hurricane, causing widespread damage, private houses, mill chimneys and Thwaites Brewery in Carr Lane were all affected.

Lengthy periods of heavy rain have caused serious flooding in the town centre in this century, and Tiplady was only too aware of the

Figure 3. Salford Bridge, a street scene at the end of the Victorian age. Tiplady did not live to see the trams (they were introduced in 1885, twelve years after his death), but he would have been familiar with the row of buildings on the left where he had his printing shop. 'Salford' means 'the ford where the willows grow' and was the site of a crossing over the River Blakewater when the Romans were here. *Author*

danger of flooding, with his shop being near the Salford Bridge. (Figure 3)

Diary 14 September 1841

About ten o'clock this evening there commenced a tremendous thunderstorm; the lightning was excessively vivid and almost continuous.

The rain fell in torrents and quickly flooded the lower part of the town. Poor Salford came in for a large share of the mud as usual.

The river was very high and many houses in the town were inundated.

Occasionally the cellars of Tiplady's shop were filled with flood water when the Blakewater was swollen by heavy rain.

Figure 4. Bolton Road Station, from a woodcut in the Blackburn Standard newspaper. *Blackburn Library*

The Railway

Britain's railway system was brand, spanking new in the 1840s, with massive development yet to come and vast fortunes to be made for some. There were 2,000 miles of track in 1843, with 5,000 more being laid by 1848. The Preston to Blackburn line was opened in 1846. (Figure 4)

Diary 1 June 1846

Glorious First! Weather most serene and splendid. On this day a new era in the history of Blackburn commenced by the formal opening of the Blackburn and Preston Railway Line.

The concourse of people witnessing the same was great, and it was truly gratifying to witness the general appearance of the line, carriages, etc.

I went to Farington, and was highly gratified with the trip.

With its company formed in 1843, there was no delay in building the line to join the North Union Railway line at Farington by early 1846. Charles recorded the delivery of his first business parcel by rail.

Tiplady clearly enjoyed everything about railways, not only as a traveller for business and pleasure, but also as a shareholder in several of the railway companies. It is sadly ironic therefore, that his son, Charles Lomax Tiplady, was killed in a rail accident in 1881, when the Manchester express, travelling at high speed, ran into the stationary train for Liverpool.

Dark Days

Blackburn's vulnerability, relying as it did on cotton, was shown in the 1860s, when the American Civil War caused a reduction of imports of raw cotton into Europe from the mainly Southern cotton-growing states. When the war began, Lancashire's cotton mills were actually overstocked with raw fibre, though within months imports of cotton had dried up. Mills across the county began short-time working. Some factories closed with disastrous consequences for the workers. In many towns, thousands were entirely dependent on the industry; household incomes dropped alarmingly.

Tiplady reflected the mood of the times.

Diary 1 January 1861

Very hard frost. Very bad printing weather.

Diary 15 February 1861

Troublous times. Lock-out on the five per cent question commenced in the Cotton Mills, when a majority of hands suspended work.

Diary 16 November 1861

First fall of snow this Winter - heavy, followed by a keen frost - times fairly gloomy; work scarce; cotton dear; money bad to get.

As winter set in, the industry was clearly declining, families began to feel the impact of lost wages and depleted savings. A Central Relief Committee was set up to alleviate distress, and this, in conjunction with local relief efforts, worked to deal with the most desperate pleas for help.

Diary 20 January 1862

Great distress in consequence of the American War. A soup kitchen established in the town.

This was in Cleaver Street, a rudimentary kitchen with two boilers preparing soup. By 3 February 1862, 2,400 quarts of soup were being distributed each day, with a distribution of meal and bread on alternate days. Tiplady observed that short-time working was almost universal.

Diary 10 February 1862

Delivery of loaves, 1,100; meal, nine loads.

Diary 5 March 1862

Heavy fall of snow. The distress of the Operatives continues; and relief is afforded to thousands of unemployed poor.

It was estimated that 30,000 out of a population of 62,126 were receiving relief in 1862. Tiplady recorded that £200 was spent on soup, bread and meat for the unemployed cotton hands in Blackburn in June 1862, but pride made many refuse relief.

Aptly named the Cotton Famine, this became fixed in local folk memory as a time of great hardship. Through 1864 and 1865, Tiplady made entries in his diary about the distress. The war ended in 1865 and the industry slowly recovered.

Some Blackburn Characters

Tiplady had a long and notable career in public life as an Improvement Commissioner, a town councillor, and later as an alderman. His near contemporary George Dewhurst also served on the Improvement Commission and was elected to the Council in 1851. That apart, the two men were very different. Whilst Tiplady was a strong Conservative, Dewhurst was the most celebrated radical in the town. He was born in 1790, and worked as a reed-maker. His radical convictions were strong and he actively promoted electoral reform among his fellow workers. In 1816 he campaigned for the repeal of the Corn Laws and for an extension of the franchise.

Figure 5. Lancaster Castle, a prison for many centuries and still so today. *Editor.*

Speaking at a meeting for handloom weavers, reportedly 10,000 strong, near Burnley in 1819, he was arrested and sentenced to two year's imprisonement in Lancaster Gaol (Figure 5).

Charles's elder brother, James Lomax Tiplady, shared Dewhurst's radical views, as many did in the town. Though politically opposed, Charles recorded Dewhurst's death.

Diary 16 August 1857

George Dewhurst, Reed-Maker, Queen Street, died, aged 67 years, a well-known Radical in his day; a councillor for St Paul's Ward, buried at the Cemetery, Aug 19

Scores of similar entries appear in the diary, almost as if he was obsessed with death. The concise word portraits of these people are of real value and are an underused source for the family historian. Tiplady was certainly acquainted with Blackburn's influential and well-to-do citizens, but his diary shows us he knew people from all walks of life, particularly his former boyhood friends.

Dairy 26 September 1855

Died, Tom Edmondson, the Letter Carrier. He was in youth a schoolfellow of mine. A very sober, upright and diligent servant of the Blackburn Post Office.

Diary 1862

Died, William Yates, Esq, Ironfounder, aged 43; the son of Mr Yates, senior, founder of the firm - Also died old John Starkie, aged 71 years, and father of 25 children; he was uncle to my uncle by marriage.

Diary 3 August 1860

Died, Joshua Smithons, Esq, aged 77 years. A good Conservative, but a close-fisted gentleman.

The Diary gives a roll-call of the leading industrialists of the time, including William Kenworthy (died 1856), Robert Hopwood (died 1853), described by Tiplady as 'the most remarkable man of his day'. Another demise drew this observation:

Diary 17 July 1853

Died, aged 49, Eccles Shorrock Esq, cotton spinner, the King of Darwen, who, by dint of perserverence, rose from a humble position to a princely fortune.

In his diary, the mighty Fieldens and Hornbys rub shoulders with shopkeepers, publicans and tradesmen of various kinds. Churchmen, too, claim his attention for he was a devout Christian.

Diary 3 August 1854

This moment has departed my best and earliest friend, Dr Whittaker, Vicar of this Town.

Diary 10 August 1854

Public funeral of Dr Whittaker; from 300 to 400 gentlemen in procession. The Bishop and Clergy, the Teachers in the Sunday Schools, the Mayor and Corporation, and a great concourse of the Inhabitants. The Procession extended from the Church to the Vicarage. Very solemn and affecting Service.

John William Whittaker, Tiplady's lamented friend, was appointed to be vicar of the Parish Church in 1822, in succession to the Rev Thomas Dunham Whittaker, who had died in 1831. So many deaths he recorded resulted from accident or disease, but some had a more tragic element.

Diary January 1870

A singular fatality occurred this month in the family of Mr Bradshaw, Plumber and Glazier. Himself, his wife and a daughter died from typhoid fever within ten days.

Was Bradshaw's death a result of his work? Before antibiotics, typhoid was a scourge of urban life, infection through untreated sewage being a principal cause.

Recreations

Was life in Blackburn in the Victorian era a constant round of drudgery and toil? Many contemporary accounts suggest that it was not, there were in fact many sources of recreation. Tiplady does not seem to have been interested in fine art or the theatre, but he enjoyed music.

Diary 23 November 1848

The sublime Oratorio of 'Joshua' was performed, Mr Clough conducting, and Mr George Ellis, the band.

Tom Clough and George Ellis were founding members of the

Blackburn Choral Society, whose events were staged in the Old Assembly Room in Market Street Lane. Tiplady might have known Ellis from their mutual association with freemasonry.

Diary 7 October 1871

Soiree and Ball for the Widows and Orphans' Fund, I O F. Mr George Ellis's Band attended. He was also there for a short time. On the following morning (Sunday) Mr Ellis was seized with an apoplectic fit, and died in the course of the day. He was 54 years old, and had been at the head of the musical profession in the district, as an instrumentalist for 25 years.

Many of the bands which he had formed and taught obtained great celebrity and carried away prizes at contests held in Lancashire and Yorkshire.

One of Tiplady's rare theatrical evenings came in 1856.

Diary 3 April 1856

At theatre, and saw Mr Henry Stowe, in 'Luke the Labourer'.

Stowe was a Blackburn character, a butcher by trade with a shop in Penny Street for 40 years. He had a passion for drama and often joined the travelling companies when they performed in the town. Stowe was a large man and made the part of Luke the Labourer his own, right up to 1867, when he gave a performance at the Theatre Royal in aid of the Infirmary Fund.

Tiplady was as much an enthusiast for the unusual as anybody and was one of the crowd watching a balloon ascent in 1849.

Diary 20 August 1849

Balloon Ascent - This evening, at about half-past six (fine evening) a Balloon ascended from the Gas Works in Darwen Street. An immense concourse of people (about 25,000) witnessed the ascent. The wind was WSW and the balloon took the direction of Accrington.

Glorious as it was, this was not the first balloon seen in the town. Mr Green's balloon had been a famous event of the 1820s. Poor Green eventually fell to his death in 1828, after a flight from Cardiff, over the River Severn.

The diary gives a vivid sense of the passing of the seasons over the years, and the round of festivals, though his descriptions of the Easter Fair are often sparse and frustrating in their lack of detail, but some religious celebrations fared better.

Diary 19 June 1869

The Church of England Schools marched in procession to the Park. They were about 1400 and looked remarkably well.

Diary 25 June 1870

Saturday. The Annual Procession of the Church Schools took place this day. The weather was fine and the assembly magnificent. The Bishop, Clergy, Churchwardens, Mayor and Teachers walked in the Procession. Numbers estimated at 15,000.

The great Lancashire celebration is, of course, the Preston Guild, held every twenty years, which Tiplady attended in 1822, 1842 and 1862.

Diary September 1842

Preston Guild. It has been my lot now to attend two Preston Guilds, being present at the one held in 1822. I do not consider there was the same attraction this time as on the last. With respect to the number of visitants, I think they were more numerous than at any previous Guild, though there was a sad falling off in Nobility.

The Trades, as usual, paraded the town with suitable devices. I walked with the Letterpress Printers. On the Friday I took my little son to see a procession of Scholars, and a most pleasing sight it was to see from 5,000 to 6,000 Scholars, all marshalled in due order, with the clergy at their head. They assembled in the Marketplace, around the Obelisk.

Tiplady does not seem to have had any interest in sport, but he was associated with the Old Subscription Bowling Club at Cicely Hole. Football and cricket are seldom mentioned, but he was keen on horse-racing.

Diary 1844

Memorandum on Steeple-Chase - the First Blackburn SteepleChase took place in the township of Billington, March 30th 1840. The second, Feb 9th, 1843. The third, March 28th, 1844.

Diary 13, 14, 15 May 1861

The 13th I went to York. There was a great race on that day between 'The Flying Dutchman' and 'Voltiguer' for 1,000 guineas. I cared little for the races, yet as I was in York, I went and witnessed the exciting spectacle; 'Flying Dutchman' won by about a length. After the Races went to the Minster; had a splendid view from the Tower, embracing 50 miles; a cloudless day.

Not only was Tiplady a printer and bookseller by trade; his interest in the printed word took up his personal time as well. He took on the position of librarian (part-time) to the Blackburn Subscription Library, a private lending library, begun in 1787, and serving a limited clientele of gentlemen, professional men and townspeople.

Tiplady was elected to chair the governing body in March 1841, and one week later a special meeting was instructed to seek ways of reviving the library's fortunes. A year later the diary records a setback.

Diary 18 September 1842

I was much disappointed this night in losing the vacant situation of Librarian to the Blackburn Subscription Library; the contest lay between myself and Wm Stirrup, who defeated me by a majority of one vote. I attributed my non-success in the first place to the active opposition of Mr Thomas Clough, solicitor.

Some years later, Tiplady gives a sorry picture of the state of the Library.

Diary 27 September, 1850

Down to the Subscription Library, which I am sorry to say is in a miserable condition; in debt, without funds, and obliged to remove from the present central situation. Left at 8.30 and went down to Mr Hoole's where I inspected the plans for the new Town Hall. (Figure 6) They are very beautiful ...

By 1851 the Library had closed, its contents sold off to a Mr Johnson for £60, and the premises sold off. On 23 August 1860 a Town's

Figure 6. Only a few years after the opening of the market, work began on the new town hall. Paterson's town hall cost £30,000, a costly sum at the time. The square in front of the town hall was the venue for rallies and processions and royal visits. *Author*

Meeting formally agreed to set up a Free Library under the Public Libraries Acts, and the diary records the laying of the foundation stone in 1872.

CONCLUSION

Not only did Abram give us Tiplady's diary, he also provided a physical description of the man, invaluable because no portrait or photograph of him is known to exist.

> *Charles Tiplady was thin, and rather below middle height. His face was pale, his head somewhat square-shaped, and his hair, which he did not lose in old age, was iron-gray . . . His gait was characteristic; he walked with his head forward, and eyes bent downward, as if intent upon his business; his walk was plodding, and marked at each step by a slight nod of his head, as I might so describe the movement.*

Abram immortalises Tiplady's habit of saying 'very proper', a phrase he used frequently and which became a source of humour in the town.

Tiplady describes an election riot in 1841, when the *Old Bull Hotel*, headquarters of the Conservative cause, was attacked by a rival political mob. Tiplady was one of the Tory supporters forced to take cover in fear of his life, as others bolted over rooftops and into cellars. His first-hand report is deservedly repeated in many histories of Blackburn, as is the remark credited to him, that he could remember Blackburn when there were only six factory chimneys to be seen, compared with 120 visible in 1866. His authoritative local knowledge was frequently called upon to settle disputes. His almanac of Blackburn events was first published in 1834.

The last entries in the diary were made on 13 and 20 September, 1873, recording the deaths of two old Blackburn townsmen. His own death was only a few weeks away, on 15 October.

On a cold, wet Autumn day, his funeral was held at the Blackburn Cemetery, attended by an official detachment of the Borough Police, the Mayor and Corporation and large numbers of people who had known and respected Charles Tiplady, sometime diarist.

9. Out on Loan: Popular Reading in Blackburn and Darwen

by Dr Robert J Snape

Introduction

A VISITOR TO BLACKBURN OR DARWEN, or indeed any northern industrial town, could hardly fail to be impressed by the grandeur of the civic buildings of the pre - 1914 era. Their scale embodies a statement of the importance the Victorians and Edwardians attached to local government and the civic ideal. While town halls occupied pride of place in terms of grandiosity, public libraries were often next in size and magnificence, and in some cases were themselves a town's finest public building, embodying a borough's commitment to culture and the arts - Preston's Harris Library and Museum being perhaps the finest example. Darwen's public library remains as one of its best civic buildings (Figure 1), and Blackburn's current converted shop premises are much inferior to what was the impressive Victorian library, museum and art gallery on Library Street (Figure 2).

Should the visitor enter Blackburn or Darwen public library and browse through the local newspapers of the pre-1914 years he would be similarly impressed by the extensive column inches of news and correspondence concerning these libraries. What libraries did, what

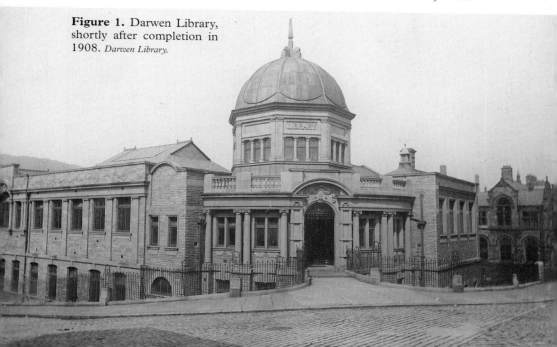

Figure 1. Darwen Library, shortly after completion in 1908. *Darwen Library.*

people read and what types of books were to be placed in libraries were important public issues in a way that they are not today. Few issues aroused greater controversy than what came to be known as 'The Great Fiction Question', which was in the first instance a simple matter of whether libraries, as rate-supported institutions, should provide fiction. As many commentators of the period remarked, if free novels on the rates, why not free swimming baths? However, the Great Fiction Question was more complex, for it raised the issue of what types of fiction should be stocked - literary novels of high cultural status and moral truth or racy sensation novels disliked by critics but loved by the reading public? There was, for example, a widely held view that fiction presenting vice or immorality would corrupt the reader, typified in the *Saturday Review's*[1] description of popular novels as carriers of 'moral poison'. Other critics felt that amusement for its own sake was intrinsically wrong, and that novels ought to educate and instruct in addition to providing for the reader's recreational needs. Conversely, novels of critically approved status within the literary canon were believed to promote civilised values, to maintain

Figure 2. Blackburn Library, Museum and Art Gallery in Library Street. *Blackburn Library.*

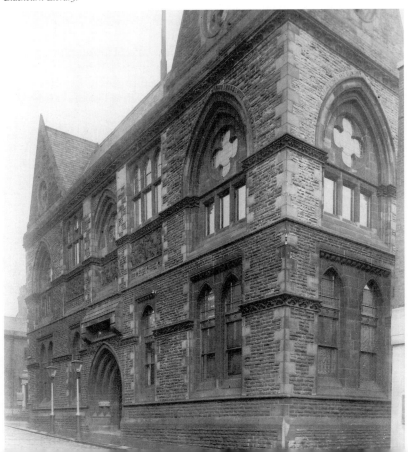

morality and to endorse the established social structure. Even books by authors recognised as literary giants were subject to condemnation if they transgressed this imaginary line, notable examples being Thomas Hardy's *Tess of the D'Urbervilles* and *Jude the Obscure*.

The Great Fiction Question split the library profession into sharply opposed camps. Many librarians were antagonistic to the provision of popular fiction in libraries, seeing it as a nuisance which interrupted the educational elements of their work. A vocal minority felt that public libraries should not provide any fiction at all and were supported in this by a small coterie of *laissez faire* political thinkers from the extreme right. Others were more liberal in their approach, and took the view that as publicly funded services, libraries should reflect the wishes and demands of all their members and provide recreational reading for their communities. As the library pioneer Thomas Greenwood wrote, why should the thousands of working class readers who depended on public library fiction for their amusement be denied this simple pleasure?[2]

There were, then, sharply opposing opinions on library fiction[3] and these are clearly in evidence in the development of the public library services of Blackburn and Darwen. Before examining these two libraries more closely, it is worth taking into account the context in which late Victorian and Edwardian libraries operated. The first *Public Libraries Act* was passed only in 1850, and even this was permissive; it was not until 1964 that town councils had by law to provide a public library service. Nevertheless most towns, particularly those in the north of England, did so; Blackburn opened its library in 1862 and when Darwen followed suit in 1871 it was the first Local Board to adopt the Free Libraries Acts. Although the rationale for the establishment of public libraries was often based upon their educational benefits and the access to text books they would afford to working people, the reality, once libraries opened their doors to the public, was that most of the books borrowed were taken for the purpose of recreational reading. Hardly anywhere did fiction represent less than 60 per cent of the total number of books issued and proportions of 80 per cent were not uncommon. Records of issues show clearly that library users at both Blackburn and Darwen preferred to borrow novels, though as will be shown below, this prompted different responses in the two towns. While the use of libraries predominantly for leisure purposes is nowadays taken as a matter of course, it was a matter of widespread social concern in the period 1850-1914. Before radio, cinemas and television, reading was one of the major pastimes for millions of people, and a huge publishing industry rapidly grew to meet the demand by producing an unprecedented amount of romances, adventure stories, penny fiction and serialised magazine fiction. What people read became the focus of an extensive social debate, and libraries, as providers of reading through public funds, were inextricably involved in this debate. It is of some interest that the books to be bought for the library were chosen by a council sub-committee, not by librarians, such was the importance attached to this task. As committees varied in their membership from town to town, differing criteria prevailed and the practice of book selection would frequently reflect the social composition of the committee.

Blackburn

From its beginning Blackburn Library reacted positively to the demand for fiction in its lending department. In the first few years fiction accounted for roughly 60 per cent of the issue and by the later 1870s this proportion had increased to 85 per cent. Even this is not the complete picture, for the reference department too lent novels on an expansive scale; for example, in 1865 it issued Mary Braddon's *Lady Audley's Secret* 53 times, Wilkie Collins' *The Woman in White* 52 times and Charles Dickens' *The Pickwick Papers* 49 times. Indeed, when at one stage the poor rate of use of the reference department was questioned in committee, the suggested remedy was not to stimulate a public demand for educational books but to increase its stock of novels. (Figure 3). In 1869 the librarian, David Geddes, noted in his annual report that:

Figure 3. Blackburn Reference Library in the 1920's. *Blackburn Library*

In popular literature the demand has been greatly in excess of the supply...the works of Dickens, Bulwer Lytton, Mayne Reid, Marryat, Lever, Scott, Disraeli, Cooper, Mrs. Henry Wood and other popular authors, are literally read to pieces, although there are more than one copy of some of the popular volumes in the library [4]

and again in 1871 commented that the demand for fiction was such that it was nearly always necessary to reserve the most popular titles. The library committee's response to the public's seemingly insatiable appetite for romances and adventure stories was to buy as many of these as possible to meet the demand. Their primary objective was that the public library should be a popular and well used institution, even though this necessitated the purchase of multiple copies of popular novels at the expense of literary fiction.

In 1890 Richard Ashton, the librarian, in an interview published in the *Preston Herald* [5] described how there was very little demand for any books other than those of fiction, history or travel, and reported that the most popular novelists were Rider Haggard, Marion Crawford, Grant Allen, Hall Caine, Edna Lyall, Mary Braddon and Emma Worboise. Although few of these names are remembered today, it is important to realise that they were the most popular writers of the day, whose works were ignored or commented upon disapprovingly by critics but eagerly devoured by millions of readers. The practice of supplying recreational reading in the reference department continued apace at this time; titles such as the Boy's Own Paper, Hood's Comic Annual, Chatterbox and the Girl's Own, Judy's Annual and the Magazine of Short Stories were all in heavy demand.

By the 1890s the committee realised - and annual reports provided some statistical substance to their belief - that the total issues from the library, then as now used as the primary quantitative measure of their effectiveness, rose or fell in unison with the pattern of novel purchases. Thus the addition to the library, between 1890 and 1895, of exceptionally large numbers of popular novels by, *inter alia*, Emma Worboise, Wilkie Collins, James Payn, Mayne Reid and Harrison Ainsworth resulted in a massive rise in the issue from 55,702 to 118,463. However, in the following four years the quantity of new fiction purchases fell after Samuel Crossley was elected to the chairmanship of the library committee, and the issue dropped to 82,981. Crossley was a Blackburn man by birth, became a successful solicitor with a practice in the town, and joined the Library Committee as a Conservative in 1894. His energies were directed primarily towards the development of the art gallery and the staging of exhibitions of natural history, and he clearly had an interest in the educational aspects of his committee's brief. In the years immediately after the turn of the century continuing reductions in the fiction issues, brought about primarily by Crossley's personal wish to see the library visited for more instructive uses, resulted in a further fall in the library's popularity which was sufficiently serious to prompt the establishment of a special committee to investigate the cause of decline. The advice of this working committee was to remedy the decline in the use of the library by establishing delivery stations in the town's working class residential areas. These were basically simple forms of branch library from which books could be ordered from the Central Library. Not surprisingly, the predominant demand was for fiction for fireside reading and by 1908 the eight delivery stations established had an average fiction issue of 95 per cent. When added to the library's total issues, these maintained the rate of fiction borrowing at 75 per cent - 85 per cent until the outbreak of war in 1914, enabling Blackburn's public library service to continue to offer an attractive service to its readers which was based primarily on the bulk provision of fiction for recreational reading.

Darwen

Although in terms of its management Darwen Library (Figure 4) has been subsidiary to Blackburn for the last quarter century, it was, before the 1914-18 war, one of the most progressive public libraries in the country, developing facilities and services much superior to those provided in Blackburn library. For example it was as late as the 1890s that public libraries began to allow readers direct access to the books, and when, in 1895, Darwen library adopted this practice, it was only the third library in the country to do so, and the first in the north of England. Blackburn readers had to wait several years before they too were accorded this facility. Darwen was also in advance of Blackburn in terms of its library building, its 1908 Carnegie-sponsored library being designed to accommodate both open access and a theatre to facilitate evening library lectures, thus providing a focal point for educational and literary activities in the town. Darwen's librarians too were at the forefront of their profession and featured frequently in professional affairs and many gained a national reputation, whereas Blackburn's librarians rarely figured in the professional press.

However, it was in its policies of fiction provision that Darwen differed most sharply to Blackburn. Book selection was the responsibility of a sub committee, but a singular feature of Darwen's selection committee was its collective degree of literary expertise, many of its members being officers of the Darwen Literary Society. While the committee generally sanctioned the purchase of several popular novels, it also explored several ways of encouraging readers to borrow literary fiction, for example by allowing borrowers to take an additional book to the standard complement, providing that the extra book was drawn from 'the higher classes of literature'. However, the latitude in fiction selection changed with the appointment to the chair of the library committee of Ralph Yates. In 1901 Yates adopted a radical stance to reduce even further the use of the library as a source of popular fiction. In February of that year he gave an address to the Darwen Literary Society in which he reported that there was an exceptionally heavy demand for popular novels and romances in the

Figure 4. Darwen Library entrance hall in 1908. *Darwen Library*

library which had resulted in fiction accounting for 84 per cent of the issue. This, he said, was damaging the image of the library, and attributed it to the commercially driven publishers who churned out new novels in quick succession to satisfy the vast market for fiction. The solution, he suggested, might be for Darwen Library to stop buying new novels - excepting those of 'undoubted repute'. Very shortly after this the Darwen Library Committee did precisely this, and although Yates at various times presented the decision as one taken for economic reasons, his address to the Literary Society betrays other motives.

The library committee announced its decision to Darwen's full town council in robust terms, Yates declaring that the library intended to make a stand against buying any book simply because it was asked for, and reporting that while any book of 'approved standard' would be bought for the library, the prevailing novel of the day, the 'puerile trash that was simply the craze of the moment', would not be found.[7] In effect, the Darwen Library Committee had appointed itself as a censor, prepared to refuse to buy for the public library any novel which, in its opinion, did not conform to some unspecified literary or cultural standard. There was an immediate reaction in the local press, the Darwen Gazette commenting thus:[8]

Who are the majority of the people who go for books? Working folks who go simply to find something to pass the leisure hours in a pleasant way. They have no burning wish for culture, or to acquire literary precision. They pay rates either directly or indirectly to secure the book they want, but here are a body of gentlemen who are taking the initiative of refusing to give it to them,

and concluded that if judged by the standard that a public library was for the purpose of providing pleasant recreation to working people in their leisure time, Yates and his committee were in the wrong. Library users too were affronted by the committee's seeming disregard for their wishes and expressed their feelings eloquently in correspondence to the local newspapers. As one put it

one may well ask, not whether this novel or that novel is worth buying, but rather who has constituted the few members of the Library Committee as the judges of what is or what is not readable? Reading is a matter of taste, and the ordinary working man and working woman prefers the novel for his or her leisure to any other kind of book. The average person who likes a bit of reading on Sundays has neither the time or the inclination to develop a literary faculty, what is wanted is an easy pleasurable bit of fiction. The Library Committee say no! [9]

The practice of not buying new popular fiction was adhered to for a number of years but was gradually relaxed under the guise of improvements in the available budget. However, the library committee remained active in its attempts to encourage readers to abandon romances and adventure stories for literary fiction. In 1901 a series of evening library lectures was established with the aim, in the words of Walter Rae, the librarian, of encouraging library users to read something other than popular fiction, and in 1905 Darwen Library became a member of the National Home Reading Union, an organisation which encouraged the formation of local reading circles at which the public could come together to read prescribed books under the guidance of a leader. In both these areas it was common for members of the library committee to take an active and participating interest. There is however little if any evidence to suggest that this initiative had any appeal to working class readers and neither is there anything to indicate that it exercised the hoped for impact on the demand for popular fiction. Darwen was also fortunate in that the librarians of the time, notably Walter Rae and Joseph Pomfret, were committed in almost a missionary sense to the role of the library service in elevating the reading patterns of the public. Pomfret was an active and enthusiastic supporter of the library's association with the National Home Reading Union and frequently addressed its meetings; as he wrote in a professional article in 1911:

> *the work of libraries in the dissemination of knowledge through books is a most important part of education and the better guidance we can give our fellows in the matter of reading, the more valuable and lasting will that work be.......I am sometimes tempted to think that books are too cheap today, for with the good which has come with the cheapness, has also come an astonishing development in the evil, weak and trashy type of book.* [10]

Darwen Library thus differed markedly from Blackburn Library insofar as at Darwen there was a primary objective of encouraging borrowers to read literary fiction and improving literature, whereas at Blackburn it was seen to be more important to allow borrowers maximum access to the popular novels they wanted to read.

Conclusion

The reasons for the differences between the approach to fiction in Blackburn and Darwen public libraries are complex, but the chief factor is based upon the character and composition of the respective library committees. In the period under discussion, local government committees were far more actively involved in the practical aspects of service than is the case today, and this applied to libraries no less than to any other area of municipal work. For example, many aspects of library management nowadays considered too trivial for reporting to committee were often recorded in detail in the minutes. A further illustration of this pattern is that in his period as chairman of the Blackburn Library Committee, Samuel Crossley wrote the annual reports himself, a task which was nearly everywhere delegated to the librarian. As was stated above, it was normal practice for the library's stock of books to be selected by a book selection sub-committee rather than by the librarian, as would be the case today, and it is thus to the committee rather than the librarian that we must turn for an explanation of the libraries' policies.

The outstanding feature of local government in Blackburn was the dominance of the Conservative party and the alliance between the council and the Church of England. As with the full town council, the Conservatives held sway on the library committee, and the library's approach to fiction provision fits within the context of a tradition of paternalist relationships between Blackburn manufacturers and employees. This paternalism was partly founded upon a perception of a shared economic dependency on cotton and was strengthened by the provision of a varied range of leisure opportunities. Works excursions, factory reading rooms, mill sports teams and other work based social events were typical ways in which large employers provided some aspects of leisure provision for their workforce, and although some degree of self-interest no doubt underpinned the motivation for this provision, the outcome was nevertheless one which benefited the recipients. As was the case in so many industrial towns, there was considerable overlap in Blackburn between economic and political leadership, with many manufacturers and factory owners having seats on the council. This facilitated a repetition of the paternalist outlook such men often bore towards their workers, and so if fiction was what the public wanted from their library, this was tacitly accepted with little dissent. Certainly the Blackburn Library Committee did not display any noticeable desire to promote literary fiction or to work towards improving the reading habits of the borrowers. This philosophy is neatly encapsulated in an article published in the Fortnightly Review by William Abram, Blackburn's first librarian and later a member of the Library Committee, (Figure 5) in which he compared the moral responsibility of a municipal authority to that of mill owners

Figure 5. W A Abram, Blackburn's first librarian. *Blackburn Library*

in terms of the health and happiness of its citizens:[11]

> *Outside the mill, too, the operative is not uncared for. The lavish provision of public parks, pleasure grounds, baths and free libraries in all the larger Lancashire towns, testifies that the corporate authorities are not unmindful of their obligations to promote the health, happiness and culture of the industrial orders.*

The *laissez faire* approach to fiction provision adopted by the Blackburn library committee was one way in which employers, through the agency of municipal influence, were able to promote this.

The composition of the Darwen Library Committee was radically different. It was controlled by the Liberals, but perhaps more significantly contained a high proportion of Congregationalists. The denominational character is important as the concept of the civic gospel, a belief that a municipal body had a mission to provide for the moral and social welfare of its community in addition to its physical needs, was engendered within the Congregational church. It originated in mid-nineteenth century Birmingham in the non-conformist ideal of practised Christianity preached by George Dawson, Robert Dale and later by Joseph Chamberlain. Dale urged Congregationalists to become involved in public affairs as aldermen and councillors, and Dawson too spoke of the missionary inspiration of the gospels in municipal administration. Congregationalists were particularly conscious of the importance of using leisure time in constructive and improving ways, and their churches developed extensive provision of leisure opportunities - sewing circles, Pleasant Sunday Afternoons, discussion groups, walking parties and rambles, picnics, games and many similar pursuits. Reading was also considered to be an excellently rational pastime, and as the *Duckworth Street Congregational Church Monthly Magazine* noted in 1907, it was 'delightful on the evening after the holidays to see the Public Library crowded with eager book selectors'.[12]

Given the domination of the Library Committee by the town's most prominent Congregationalists, it is not surprising that the management of Darwen's library was approached through the perspective of the civic gospel. Many of the library committee's more senior members were, in addition to being Congregationalists, members of the Darwen Literary Society, and thus had an active interest in novels and their reading. It was not uncommon for those who were members of both the library committee and the Literary Society to deliver library lectures on books and literature, and it is easy to imagine the distaste such men might have had for a library service dominated by popular and sensational fiction. In no-one was the blend of Congregationalism, a love of literary culture and personal drive more clearly embodied than in Ralph Yates, the committee's chairman. Yates, a Darwen man by birth, was one of the town's most charismatic figures and in addition to having a long political career on the town council was also a founding member and later a president of the Literary Society, and a man of highly cultivated intellectual and literary interests. Darwen's library service effectively became an expression of the values of Yates and his committee, most of whom shared his interests and his religious principles. Even the National Home Reading Union, so eagerly espoused by the Darwen committee as a means of encouraging the reading of a better category of popular fiction, was established by a Congregationalist, John Brown Paton, thus further emphasising the denominational associations of the committee.

The First World War brought the debate of the fiction question to a close and although after the War the provision of fiction in public libraries continued to be a perennial topic of discussion within the library profession, it never again reached the intensity described above, nor did it figure largely in the general discourse on popular recreation. Blackburn's and Darwen's libraries grew and developed services which were eventually little different to each other and in 1974 both were subsumed within the Lancashire County Library service before becoming Blackburn with Darwen Library in 1997. As society in general has grown more liberal in its outlook there has been a gradual relaxation in peoples' attitudes to books, and library selection policies have reflected this trend, though modern libraries have experienced some debate concerning books with allegedly racist or gender bias. A further striking difference between the present and the period covered in this chapter, however, is in the degree of social importance attached to the library as a municipal institution and in the perceptions of the potential of the library as a benefit to its local community. Libraries certainly seem to figure less in the news than was once the case, and in terms of local politics, few libraries now function as autonomous departments, most being smaller partners within education or leisure departments. Local government too has lost much of its nineteenth century missionary imperative, and remains a shadow of its former self following governmental changes in its functions over the decades. As this chapter has tried to show, it was not always thus, and the last word may be left to Joseph Pomfret, who in 1928 dedicated the town's fiftieth anniversary souvenir brochure[13] to the youth of Darwen in the hope that they would obtain a clearer idea of their civic inheritance and would come to realise the importance of local government not only to the community but also to the life of every individual citizen.

Notes and References

1. Novel reading. Saturday Review, February 1867, pp 196-7.
2. Greenwood, T., The great fiction question. *Library Year Book*, Cassell 1897, pp 107-16.
3. For a more detailed account of the national debate on the provision of fiction in libraries before 1914 see Snape, Robert *Leisure and the Rise of the Public Library*, Library Association Publishing, 1995.
4. *Blackburn Free Library Annual Report 1868-69.*
5. *Preston Herald*, 21 June 1890.
6. *Darwen News*, 13 February 1901.
7. *Darwen Gazette*, 8 June 1901.
8. ibid.
9. *Darwen Gazette* , 2 August 1902.10. Pomfret, Joseph Reading Circles, Library World, April 1911, pp 289-94.
11. Abram, W, Social condition and political prospects of the Lancashire workmen. *Fortnightly Review*, 1868, pp 426-41.
12. *Duckworth Street Congregational Church Monthly Magazine*, August 1907.
13. Pomfret, J *Official Souvenir of the Fiftieth Anniversary of the Incorporation of the Borough of Darwen*, 1928.

10. EXPERIENCES OF AN IMMIGRANT IN BLACKBURN

by Ashok Chudasama

I ARRIVED IN BLACKBURN ON 11 DECEMBER 1964 It was cold. It was bleak and, living up to its name, it was black: the buildings were all black, the many mill chimneys were all black, my future seemed black (Figure 1). In the town centre the old market and clock tower were being demolished to make way for a new shopping precinct. I was amazed at the row upon row of terraced housing that seemed to go off in all directions, climbing right up to the grey sky. I stood and shivered and wished I was back in Dar Es Salaam in Tanzania with all the warmth and colour of East Africa around me.

My family came originally from Gujerat in India. My father Jethalal was a shoemaker. He emigrated to Tanzania in the early 1940's. Thousands of Asians were then being encouraged to emigrate by the British government who wanted skilled workers to help build the East African economy.

I was born, the first of five boys in Dar Es Salaam in 1946. My

Figure 1. Blackburn in the old days, a 'forest' of chimneys.
Blackburn Library

Figure 2. Peter Street in winter. This is me with a demolition site in the background soon to be occupied by high rise flats. *Author*

father's business prospered. He became an importer of footwear and related materials. I remember well the delivery of crates from Italy and Germany. My father would have me and my brothers open them up. I can remember the smell of leather to this day.

We had a big house and a big garden. There were no terraced houses in Tanzania like the ones in Blackburn. We had many servants and lived a life of ease and luxury. It wasn't to last however. Competition in the form of cheap imports from the Far East threatened our way of life. The time came when the family had to consider moving again.

Our neighbours had friends who had emigrated to England and were living in Blackburn. They encouraged us to join them. At the time the Lancashire textile industry was desperate for workers. It was decided that my brother and myself should go there first. Once we had established ourselves we could bring over the rest of the family.

Our first house was in Peter Street, a two-up-two-down terraced house with open fires, no bathroom, and an outside toilet (Figures 2-3). My first job was as a battery filler at Higham's Mill in Great Harwood. The batteries held bobbins of weft and it was my job to make sure they were kept topped up, otherwise the loom stopped and everyone lost money. I found the noise appalling. The clatter of the looms would be ringing in my ears long after I had finished my shift. I was amazed at how the women could communicate by lip-reading.

Figure 3. Number nine Peter Street, our first home which cost £200; £20 deposit and the balance over five years. This shows my mother with our family doctor Mrs Brown, my only sister and youngest brother. *Author*

I could never understand what people were saying to each other.

Actually it didn't need the din of a weaving shed to cause communication difficulties for me in those days. I had problems understanding people anyway. English was the language of the middle classes in Tanzania. I spoke it well and had not anticipated any difficulties in England. However, I wasn't prepared for the Lancashire accent. It was some time before I was familiar with its idioms and nuances. I remember calling into a shop soon after I arrived and being served by a pretty, young, English girl. 'Thanks, love,' she said, when I gave her the money for my purchase. That word love brought the colour to my cheeks, and I left in some confusion, a little alarmed at the forwardness of English girls. It was with a mixture of relief and disappointment that I later learned that in Lancashire the word 'love' is lavished on all and sundry.

I left the mill and got a job at Mullards, the electronics company, first as a process worker and later as a quality conroller, inspecting TV tubes. By this time, the rest of the family had joined us and my father was keen for me to be married. An introduction was arranged with a girl from London called Jaibharti. We got on well and were married in 1968, despite the fact that my bride missed some of the sophistication of the metropolitan life. She did like the water in Blackburn though, and always took a gallon or so down with her when she visited London.

We were living in Edmundson Street by then, again with only an open fire for warmth. My mother suffered badly from the cold, even crouched right over the fire she couldn't get warm. We decided to install central heating, quite an innovation for immigrant households in those days. A further innovation occurred when I passed my driving test and bought my first car, an Austin; no more waiting for buses on cold, winter mornings.

In 1981 we experienced our first real setback since arriving in England. Because of cheap imports from the Far East, Mullards had to make 1800 people redundant. My own job was going too, but because a large number of those being put out of work were of Asian origin, and because I had the necessary communication skills, I was kept on to help people cope with redundany, how to invest their money, how to apply for jobs, etc.

This experience stood me in good stead when I finally had to leave. My knowledge of finance enabled me to get a job as an insurance salesman. For three years I was happy and successful in the job, but the economic climate changed yet again; competition became fiercer and pressure was put on salesmen to sell policies to people regardless of whether they could afford them. I was in an impossible position. It was against all my principles to deceive people in this way. I was forced to resign.

Yet another setback, and by now it was obvious to me that despite my achievements, I was going to need some sort of paper qualification to make further progress in my career. I took an Access Course to prepare me for entry to university. I went on to do the B.A. Honours course in Applied Social Sciences at Preston Polytechnic, now the University of Central Lancashire.

Ever since the passing of the *Race Relations Act* in 1966 there had been a gradual improvement in the circumstances of immigrant communities. The uglier aspects of discrimination: the 'whites only' adverts for accommodation etc., were made illegal. Efforts were beginning to be made to address the problems of people from different backgrounds. By the time I left college progressive councils like Blackburn's were well advanced in this respect. I got a job with them, first in the Housing Department, then in Personnel, promoting equal opportunities policies, then in the Economic Development Department, and recently in the Education and Training Department as an Industry/Education Liaison Officer.

Blackburn has changed enormously since I arrived here 35 years ago. Now it is a thriving, cosmopolitan town with an exciting future. It is my home now, and for second and third generation immigrants it is the only home they have ever known. Problems remain, but I am confident they can be resolved.

My eldest son has married a girl from the English community. My family and hers have become close friends. For me this is symbolic of the closest possible integration between our communities. After all, the only real difference between us is the colour of our skin, and when all is said and done, of what consequence is that?

11. DARWEN TOWER

by Alan Duckworth

SOMETIMES IT'S PALE, SOMETIMES IT'S DARK. I've seen it look almost white against a louring sky. The Victoria Jubilee Tower over Darwen picks up the mood of the day like a speculative finger held up to test the wind.

Built of stone from the quarry at Red Delph nearby, they say imported stone would not have stood up to the climate, it glows red and golden on rare, fine days, and turns dark, almost black, when the rain comes stalking across the moors.

It was permanently black once, at one with the mill chimneys in the valley below, and shamelessly bareheaded, the original turret having blown off in a gale in 1947. In 1971 however Bill Lees, as Mayor, established a fund to have it cleaned, repaired and crowned anew in fibreglass.

Our northern hills positively bristle with follies, forts, look-out towers, cairns and beacons; from Rivington Pike to Stoodley Pike, from the Siverdale Pepperpot to Billinge Beacon. Sooner or later the urge to crown the nearest hill has proven irresistible.

In Darwen's case the idea was first put forward in a letter from W T Ashton in the *Darwen News* of 17 November 1883. The rights of the people to use the moorland footpaths were being negotiated, largely as a result of Ashton's efforts, and he wrote to suggest a tower be built from which 'telescopic observations' could be made and where refreshments could be obtained. The idea was taken up by another correspondent, who added that the tower could also stand in memory of the late James Huntington, managing partner of Potters Wallpaper manufacturers, and be known as the Huntington Tower.

It was fourteen years before the idea resurfaced in the press, in a letter in the *Darwen News* on 13 January 1897, when the writer, signing him, or herself, *Landmark*, suggested a tower as a way of celebrating Victoria's Diamond Jubilee. The idea was officially proposed by Councillor Robert Shorrock at a public meeting on 26 April that year.

A competition was held for designs for the tower. It attracted twenty one entries and that of David Ellison of Darwen Borough Engineers' Office was selected. A comparison of this (Figure 1) with the actual tower (Figure 2) shows that some modifications were made.

Tuesday 2 June 1897 was the Queen's Jubilee Day. It was hot and sunny with a cooling breeze. It was a public holiday. The bells at Darwen's Holy Trinity church began pealing at 8.00am. Outside the town hall, the police, the fire brigade, the postmen, magistrates, corporation officials and councillors assembled for the short

Figure 1. Prize winning design for the Tower. *Darwen Library*

Figure 2. Darwen Tower. *Author*

procession to Holy Trinity, where a service was to be held. Figure 3 shows the groups outside the town hall.

In the afternoon there was a gathering of school children in Market Square. Hymns were sung and the Darwen Temperance Band performed. Afterwards, the children marched off to attend galas on various fields in the town, followed by tea parties.

Later, the focus switched to the moors, where the Pickup Bank Band played until 5.00pm, when the Mayor, Alexander Carus, cut the first sod for the tower. The bells at Holy Trinity were chiming again. At 7.00pm a fairy fountain began to play in Market Square, and in the parks, bands performed until late in the evening. At 9.00pm illuminations came on throughout the town and at 10.00pm rockets were fired from the moor and the bonfire was lit.

Darwen had done full justice to the day, but it was all only an echo of another day of celebration held less than a year previously. On Saturday 5 September 1896, a procession of over 1,000 people watched by many more had left the town and reached the moor via Sunnyhurst, where Alexander Carus had declared 55 acres of the moor open and absolutely free of access and the remaining 225 acres accessible subject to certain restrictions.

Again, the bands played, there was a bonfire and there were fireworks. The *Darwen News* of 9 September 1896 made an attempt to describe the scene (Figure 4).

Figure 3. Crowds gathering outside the Town Hall. *Darwen Library*

The bonfire blazed away until 3.00am on Sunday morning and it wasn't entirely extinguished by midday. Clearly the town had felt it had something to celebrate which was every bit as important as a queen's jubilee.

Coming and going across the moors had once no more been considered a special right or privilege than had breathing or looking at the stars, but of course as soon as someone owned the land, things began to change. And they began to change dramatically when that owner realised that there was money to be made leasing the gaming rights, providing that the lower classes could be kept at bay. Gamekeepers were instructed to turn people off the moor and footpaths and bridleways were stopped.

It became a conflict involving lots of people, but two men came to represent the opposing sides. The Reverend William Arthur Duckworth, born in 1829, inherited the Manor of Over Darwen from his Uncle George, who had bought it from John Trafford in 1810. William was educated at Trinity College, Cambridge, ordained in 1854, and married to Edina Campbell, daughter of the Lord Chancellor, in 1859. William was only an occasional visitor to Darwen, living at Orchardleigh near Frome in Somerset.

On the other side was another William, William Thomas Ashton, born in Blackburn in 1832, who came to Darwen at fifteen years of age to work first at Brookside Mill, then at Bowling Green Mill, before becoming manager of Eccles Shorrock's mines at Dogshaw Clough and Entwistle Moss. He knew the moorland paths well, riding his horse over them to collect orders and settle accounts with customers. He stubbornly resisted all attempts to turn him off and, if his way was barred, would take a saw to clear it.

Others joined the struggle and on Sunday 28 July 1878, Richard Ainsworth, John Oldman,

Figure 4. Darwen News 9 September 1896. *Darwen Library*

down the Valley, voted the spectacular effect a decided success. The fireworks included: Royal ascent of signal maroons fired from iron mortars, and exploding with terrific reports. Grand illumination, with coloured fires, changing colour four times, and transforming the place to fairyland. Display of large coloured rockets. Discharge of mine serpents. Nest of golden swarmers. Discharge of mine crackers. Mortars representing the scorpions among the ants. Ascent of tourbillons, forming a cascade of fire in ascent and descent. Congreve shells, displaying a crowd of coloured stars, representing a bouquet of flowers. Set piece: Alladin's jewelled tree, commencing with a large vertical wheel with coloured centre, changing to seven wheels illuminated; and suddenly changing to Alladin's jewelled tree, with superb foliage and coloured flowering blossoms. Rocket with bright stars. Rocket with comet stars. Rockets with orange and blue stars. Rockets with red, white, and blue stars. Discharge of mine crackers. Discharge of mine serpents, with nests of hissing fiery snakes. Ascent of fiery torpedos, flying through the air with great velocity, and exploding with tremendous reports. Bomb shell, displaying the greatly admired golden cloud, intermixed with sparkling emeralds and rubies. Set Piece: Revolving war device, with many changes. Set piece: Diamond Saxon, commencing with a large rainbow wheel changing to five wheels adorned with various coloured fires displaying all the beautiful colours of the rainbow, which suddenly changes to the Diamond Saxon, with Prince of Wales' feathers, finishing with a glory of reports. Set piece: Revolving sun, commencing with a double vertical wheel with red roses in the centre, surrounded with the Royal stars of Brunswick, suddenly changing to the rising sun, with immense spray of gold and silver fire 90 feet in circumference, a very beautiful piece of pyrotechny. Rocket with bright stars. Rocket with comet stars. Rocket with crimson and purple stars. Rocket with orange and blue stars. Rocket with red, white, and blue stars. Mine of serpents. Mine of crackers. Discharge of large shells, displaying a golden cloud, then changing to an immense crystal chandelier. Whistling rockets. Rockets, with twinkling stars, "Twinkle, twinkle, little star, How I wonder what you are." Explosion of Sinbad's jewel mine. Jack in the box. Batteries of mines, with gold and silver serpents and crackers. The devil among the tailors. Flight of tourbillons, representing a Chinese umbrella. Discharge of large shells, representing a rich cornfield sprinkled with poppies. Set piece: Performing monkey, the mechanical effects of which were marvellous, causing much amusement. Rocket with bright stars. Rocket with comet stars, long fiery tales. Rocket with red and green stars. Rockets with orange and blue stars. Rockets with red, white, and blue stars. Discharge of mine crackers. Discharge of mine serpents, with nests of hissing fiery snakes. Flight of tourbillions, forming umbrellas of fire. Discharge of large shells, displaying a golden cloud, then changing to an immense crystal chandelier. Set piece: The Falls of Niagara, beautifully depicted, with a mighty roar, in immense waves of liquid fire. Grand finale: Half-circle device and motto "Good night to all," with batteries of coloured Roman candles playing in cross fires. During the evening there was a strong north-east wind blowing, and consequently the baloon which should have been let off from the Moor had to be taken down into the town. From near the market-house ascent was made, carrying a powerful magnesium light, illuminating the country for miles round, and discharging a great variety of coloured fireworks in every direction. Just a little after eight o'clock, and when the fireworks had been completed, the bonfire was lit by the three gentlemen named above, and there was very soon a blaze that could be seen for miles round. From ten o'clock on Saturday evening till three o'clock on Sunday morning the sky looked to be almost on fire with the glare. After this hour we had not the pleasure of witnessing it, but we were told that the fire was not altogether dead at noon on Sunday. This event will be long remembered by many, and the fireworks and huge bonfire will impress the event on the minds of the youth of the town.

THE MAYOR'S BANQUET IN THE EVENING.

James Fish, Ellis Gibson and Joseph Kay went on the moor to provoke a confrontation. They were intercepted at Red Delph by a band of half a dozen gamekeepers and a scuffle took place.

On 1 August 1878 the five were served with writs answerable next day at the High Court in London. It must have been hoped that legal and financial difficulties would prove a more impenetrable barrier than those erected on the moors, but, with the help of W T Ashton and solicitor Fred Hindle, affidavits were made out and John Oldman, having pawned his watch for the fare, walked to Bolton to catch the mail train.

He reached London with little time to spare and only ten minutes with his legal advisors before going into court. The judge, Sir George Jepson, dismissed the Reverend Duckworth's application for an injunction against the five on the understanding that they refrained from any sporting activity on the moor.

This was a victory, but it left the situation still unresolved and a committee was formed under the chairmanship of Ashton to carry on the campaign. Ashton died in 1894, but his sons continued the fight. It wasn't until September 1896 that negotiations were finally concluded by an agreement that granted 55 acres absolutely free, and the remaining 225 acres to become so on the death of the Reverend W A Duckworth.

Building a tower now had the added significance of staking the town's claim to the moor. Local contractor R J Whalley was engaged to build it; Messrs Coulthurst of Robert Street Foundry to do the cast iron work; Messrs Entwistle and Nutter of Market Street to do the plumbing and glazing and the town's Building Inspector to oversee the work.

It must have been a mixed blessing for the workmen having to walk up to the site every day with their tools and face the bitter winds, cold, grey skies and incessant rain that can be a feature of the weather in Darwen as much in August as it can be in December. On the other hand, they were out in the open, left to get on with it, and, when it was fine, it must have been pleasant enough, and there was always the opportunity of drawing the attention of any passing gamekeeper to how the tower was progressing.

The completed tower was an octagonal structure with outer faces fifteen feet wide. There were 65 stone steps with an iron staircase of seventeen steps leading to the top. There were sixteen windows originally fitted with plate glass. There were three panels, separated by mullions over the northern archway, the centre one bearing the shield devised for Victoria's Jubilee, that on the left describing the purpose of the tower, and that on the right listing the members of the Jubilee Committee. The shields over the other archways were left blank. The tower was built square to the compass and had outer walls two feet thick.

There was originally a turret of pitch pine and the height from the moor to the gilt ball surmounting the turret had been 86 feet. The turret was also octagonal with plate glass windows and leaded transoms. It had a moulded cornice, roofed by a lead dome, over which was a cast iron finial with wrought iron arms, indicating the points of the compass. There was a copper vane bearing the royal cipher. The finial was eight feet six inches high and was supported on the centre post of the iron staircase. It weighed four hundredweight and helped to stabilise the turret.

Nickolaus Pevsner, in his monumental work on the buildings of England, refers to it as a 'stumpy, awkwardly proportioned piece'. Viewed in isolation, this might be true, but in its context with the moors all around and the town down below, it's hard to think of any design that would look any better. It certainly isn't shamed by its fellows: the Peel Tower on Holcombe Hill, or the Pigeon Tower at Rivington, or any of the other monuments and follies further afield. None of them are works of art, and yet they all seem appropriate somehow. Perhaps we've just become accustomed to them. We don't see them for what they are, but as symbols of our heritage.

It had been hoped that £400 would meet the cost of the tower, but, as is often the case with such projects, the original estimate was far too low. The Jubilee fund raised £1,300. Over £300 went on Jubilee Day expenses. Half the remainder went to the Nursing Association to send poor people to convalesce at the seaside. Mr R J Whalley's bill came to over £700, so the balance had to be found by the Corporation and the members of the Jubilee Committee themselves.

It was inevitable too that the work should be delayed by bad weather. As can be seen in Figure 5, the porticoes around the base of the tower were still incomplete by the official opening day of 24 September 1898. For the third year running the town's people were making their way up on to the moors for a ceremony closely associated with the right to roam freely up there. By 3.30 in the afternoon, over 3,000 people were assembled around the tower. They must have watched it being built from down below in the town, but for many this must have been the first time they'd seen it at close quarters.

The police were there in force under Inspector Whittaker and the red uniforms of the 1st Volunteer Battalion of the East Lancashire Regiment brought some colour to the scene. The Darwen Band was playing at Stockport, so the Blackburn Volunteer Band was in attendance.

The key to the tower was engraved with the arms of Darwen, and on one side with the inscription: 'Queen Victoria's Diamond Jubilee. Darwen celebrations 1897', and on the other: 'The Tower erected in Commemoration on Darwen Moor, opened by Rev W A Duckworth MA, Lord of the Manor September 24th 1898'. This key was presented to the Reverend W A Duckworth so that he could declare the tower open.

What was Duckworth doing there? He hadn't been to the previous two ceremonies, and the trip up from Somerset's no joke even today,

Figure 5. Opening ceremony, incomplete porticoes can be seen in the background. *Darwen Library*

with all the road-works on the M6, it must have been worse then, even if the trains did run on time. Had he run out of excuses, or had he at last got used to the idea that he had lost, and had finally stopped grinding his teeth long enough to be able to make a speech?

He certainly used the opportunity to express his fears that his tenant's, Mr Ashworth's, grouse shooting was going to suffer and to express the hope that people would cause as little disturbance to the game as possible, especially during the mating season. Ashworth was absent, but Duckworth read a note from him conveying his good wishes and echoing the hope that trespass would be less in the coming season than it had been in the last.

It fell to Fred Hindle to make the vote of thanks, in which he declared his opinion that the moors were the undoubted and rightful inheritance of the people of Darwen. Perhaps the undercurrents of ill-feeling had unsettled them, but before the Mayor, Mr Huntington, could speak, the Band launched into the national anthem, which they played to the end. Mr Huntington then made his speech, and the Band played the national anthem again.

And there the tower is, over 100 years later, with every reason to suppose that it will be there 100 years hence and even longer. Of course it doesn't do to make confident assertions like that; Fate is fond of confounding them. During the Second World War there was some agitation to have the tower dismantled lest it prove a landmark for German bombers, and in 1974 the town's General Purposes Committee received an offer for the tower from an American who wanted to transfer it to his ranch. They declined to even consider it.

Darwen and its tower belong together now. It's impossible to think of the town without an image of the tower flickering in the mind. Of all such towers and monuments only Blackpool's stands for its town in quite the same way. It might not be a brilliant piece of architecture, but it's been painted, drawn and photographed countless times. It's been reproduced in gold and silver by jewellers, and recently in baser metal to decorate the railings in the town centre. It has figured on plates and postcards and tea-towels. It's well loved because it belongs to everybody and nobody.

It isn't there to remind us of Queen Victoria; in fact quite the opposite. Quite brilliantly it flaunts a triumph for the common people in the guise of a loyal gesture. It stands for the rights of workers and others to escape from their narrow streets and lives and get a breath of fresh air. It stands for commonality. It stands for freedom. May it stand for a very long time to come.

12. A History of the Roman Catholic Church in Blackburn

by Stephen Martin Child

HOW IT ALL BEGAN. In the year 180AD, York had a Catholic Bishop, and the faith of the people might be gathered from the faith of their bishop. This is interesting to us because Blackburn and its neighbourhood might have been in the diocese or archdiocese of York. The ecclesiastical divisions of the country often coincided with the civil and the miltary (Roman) divisions. Ribchester was a Roman centre and, at a later date, Ribchester was within the deanery of St Anne's, Blackburn. The Roman road from Manchester to Ribchester went through the centre of Blackburn, and a Roman road passed from Ribchester to York. So it might be that Roman Catholicism started in Blackburn about the year 180AD.

Since the Reformation, Lancashire has been the centre of English Catholicism. In the sixteenth century, the Protestant Reformation turned Catholicism, which had previously commanded universal assent in England, into a minority religion. However, with a long struggle, it survived. With the Industrial Revolution, Catholic Lancashire grew even stronger, especially as it was reinforced by Irish immigrants.

An official survey of recusancy (refusing to attend the Protestant church) in 1596 noted that there were 61 such people in Blackburn, which was a higher figure than a lot of other towns in Lancashire. On the eve of the Civil War in 1642, Parliament ordered all adult males to take a protestation of loyalty to King and Parliament and the Protestant religion. The number of refusals indicated the strength of Catholicism. In Blackburn, the number of refusals was 225 (9.5 per cent of the population).

In the eighteenth century, Lancashire Catholics worshipped in the domestic chapels of the gentry, and the new chapels built by the Catholic congregations and their clergy. In 1770, in Blackburn, mass was celebrated in Wensley Fold in the house of the millowner John Anderton. The Andertons built and owned the first cotton factory in Blackburn. During the late eighteenth century, weavers predominated amongst the Catholics of Blackburn Deanery.

From 1773, there was Mass once a month in a small chapel

contained in a house on Old Chapel Street, near Penny Street. This was really the start of St Alban's Church.

In 1780, a widow named Mrs Mary Hodgson of Little Plumpton left £400 for the building of a new Catholic chapel in Blackburn. One of her sons, the Reverend John Hodgson, a priest at Clayton-le-Moors, helped forward the project by opening the first chapel in what are now the two cottages, Number sixteen and eighteen Chapel Street, near the former chapel of 1773.

In 1781, the Reverend William Dunne, DD, came to Blackburn as the first resident priest in the town after the Reformation. He occupied the back part of a house at 47 King Street. The second chapel was between Chapel Street and King Street, and it opened in 1781. In 1793, there were 26 baptisms in this Catholic Chapel, and in 1804 there were about 745 Catholics in the town. On 27 October, 1805. Reverend William Dunne died suddenly while saying Mass. It was another year before the next priest was appointed, Father Fletcher. During the interim, Catholics attended Mass at the private chapel of Mr Petre at Dunkenhalgh. Distance was obviously no obstacle to Catholics in those days.

A census of Catholics was taken in 1819 and there were 1,200 Catholics in Blackburn and surrounding districts. The population in 1821 in Blackburn was 21,940.

In 1824, work began on building a new church and in 1826, the congregation moved from Chapel Street to their third chapel at Larkhill. Henceforward, the church was publicly known as St Alban's.

Education

The first Catholic approach for government funds involved a test case (in about 1838) for a grant towards the Catholic school at Blackburn. By 1818 there was a Catholic Sunday School in Blackburn, and by 1820 there existed a free school with a full time lay teacher. A Catholic teacher and pupils walked in the procession for the Coronation of William IV, and they did so again, placed between the Presbyterians and the Methodists, in 1838, for the Coronation of Queen Victoria. The school was partly financed by annual sermons, which in 1834 were supported by Blackburn Choral Society. In 1850, the Catholic millowners John and Thomas Sparrow established a factory school where the Catholic children were given religious instruction. In the same year, the Notre Dame nuns arrived to take over the parochial schools. In Blackburn in 1866 24 girls presented themselves for examinations as pupil teachers; only two boys presented themselves.

The Catholic Conference

An annual conference was held each year, beginning in 1888. The first one was held at Westminster in London. In 1905, it came to Blackburn, and was held from Sunday 24 September to Thursday 28 September. On the Sunday there were Masses and special sermons; on Monday a public meeting and concert; on Tuesday, the actual conference; Wednesday was a rest day, and on Thursday excursions were arranged to Stonyhurst, Whalley and Mitton, or Whitewell, or Bolton Abbey.

THE CHURCHES

Christ the King and St Anthony, Shadsworth

This church reflects the huge number of houses built in the Shadsworth area in the 1950s It opened in 1959. The Church of the Good Shepherd, Earl Street, opened on 13 July 1967, this church was built to serve the Wimberley Street area, an existing large housing area. This was unusual because most of the other churches built during this period were erected to cater for new housing areas. It started as a chapel-of-ease for St Alban's.

Holy Souls, Brownhill

This church opened in 1925, and serves the eastern outskirts of the town.

Our Lady of Perpetual Succour, Longshaw

Yet another church to be opened in the 1950s or 1960s because of new housing estates being built. This church serves the Longshaw and Higher Croft areas. It opened on 18 September 1955, and is dedicated to Our Lady of Perpetual Suffering. It cost about £25,000 to £30,000 to build. Four hundred pounds was raised by the new parish priest, Father V Flannery. He spent countless hours calling on his parishioners and piling their contributions (old gas ovens, boilers, scrap metal, milk bottle tops, paper, etc) into his small car and taking them to the merchants' yards.

The Church was opened by the Vicar-Capitular of the Salford Diocese, Monsignor J Cunningham. It is built in a modernist style on high ground off Pilmuir Road. A parish hall was constructed underneath the nave. Interestingly, the fourteen stations of the Cross on the walls were painted by Father R Brierley a curate at St Joseph's Church.

Figure 1. Drawing of Pleasington Priory. *Author*

Pleasington Priory (Figure 1)

This is a Grade One listed building, one of only two in the Borough of Blackburn with Darwen the other one being Turton Tower. The foundation stone was laid on 6 June 1816, and the work was finished, and the church opened on 24 August 1819. It is dedicated to St Mary and St John the Baptist. It was the gift of the then Squire of Pleasington Hall, John Francis Butler. The public house across the road is called *The Butlers Arms.*

There is a tradition that J F Butler had a serious accident on the site of the present church and was very nearly killed. He there and then resolved to erect a church on the identical spot, in thanksgiving for his marvellous escape.

The architect of the Priory was John Palmer, and it cost more than £20,000 to build. Palmer achieved the remarkable feat of incorporating within its design every form of architecture from Early English to Regency Gothic. The Priory was built by one sculptor, three stone workers, four builders, two labourers and two carters. The church is 115 feet long, 48 feet wide and 86 feet high.

St Paul's, Feniscowles

This is a sub-church of Pleasington Priory and was built in response to the huge number of houses erected in Feniscowles in the 1950s and

1960s It was built by Messrs Whittaker & Co of Blackburn, at a cost of about £25,500. It was completed in March 1968. The Church was called St Paul's because 1968 was the Year of St Paul, and it was also the name of the then Pope. The church was officially opened on 5 May 1968 by His Excellency, the Apostolic Delegate.

Sacred Heart
At the end of the last century the western side of Blackburn was developing and a new Catholic church was needed in addition to St Anne's. A site was accordingly acquired at the corner of St Silas's Road and Leamington Road. On Saturday 5 May 1900, the foundation stone was laid for a chapel-of-ease to St Anne's. In January 1901, the building was finished. A first it was only used as a school. It cost £2,579 13s 8d to build. Mass was said for the first time on 17 February 1901. On Sunday 14 July 1901 the Church was solemnly dedicated to the Sacred Heart by Bishop Bilsborrow Mass was only said on Sunday at the chapel-of-ease in the early years. All other functions, eg weekday masses, confessions, baptism, etc, were said at St Anne's.

On 29 October 1905, Sacred Heart ceased to be a chapel-of-ease and began its existence as a separate church and parish. When the debt was finally paid off for the building in 1918 thoughts turned to building a new church. A site was acquired at the junction of Preston New Road and Billinge Avenue. The foundation stone was laid on 9 October 1937 by Bishop Henshaw and it was opened on Sunday 25 September 1938. It is of Gothic design by Messrs E B Norris and F M Reynolds of Stafford and Manchester. The cost was about £12,000.

St Alban's (Figures 2-3)
The building of the new church (the third one) began in 1824. In 1823, the Larkhill site had been bought from Joseph Birley a mill owner. The purchase price of the land was £1,260 3s 9d The new church was opened on Thursday 22 June 1826 by the Right Reverend Dr Painswick Bishop of the Northern District. The Church was plain, chapel-like, unpretentious, built in brick and stone facings, with three very handsome entrances in the Ionic style of architecture. Long narrow windows on both sides of the building admitted plenty of light. There was seating for about 750. The grounds were used as a burial ground for Catholics until 1860.

A striking feature of the interior was the high altar, a large circular entablature on six massive Corinthian pillars and lighted from a glass

Figures 2 - 3. St.Alban's Church. *Blackburn Library*

dome or lanterns rising high above the building; it was a landmark from many places about the town.

The span of the roof was always considered a dangerously wide one and the 1890s it proved to be a real danger. This fact accelerated the building of a new one.

An organ and a gallery for the choir was provided in 1835.

The demolition of the old church began on 16 May 1898. For the next three years, mass was celebrated in St Alban's Parochial Hall. On 15 October 1898 John Bilsborough, Bishop of Salford, laid the foundation stone of the new church, and on 8 December 1901, it was finally opened. The architect was Edward Goodie, a Catholic from London. The total building cost was £40,000. A huge bazaar was held from 16 October to 21 October 1901 in the Exchange Hall, now the Apollo Cinema, to celebrate the opening.

The church is built of Yorkshire stone. The style of architecture is fourteenth century Gothic, but the chancel is fifteenth century Gothic.

St Anne's

St Anne's Church, France Street, was opened in 1849, but on Saturday 4 July 1925, the foundation stone of a new church was laid by the Reverend William Shine. The church opened on Christmas Eve 1926 at Midnight Mass. It is built in the Lombard Romanesque style and, significantly, it contains sixteen Monolith Siena and Briscia pillars. It cost about £7,500 to build.

St John Vianney, Livesey

The Bishop of Salford, the Right Reverend G A Back, dedicated a new Roman Catholic church hall, on Livesey Branch Road, to St John Vianney on 12 April 1962. It started as a daughter church of St Peter's Mill Hill, and it cost £11,500.

St Joseph's, Audley

St Joseph's Church started as a new mission in three cottages, given by Mr R Shakeshaft, in William Hopwood Street, in 1869. The foundation stone of the first church was laid on Whit Monday, 1875, and the Church was opened by Cardinal Manning on 3 August 1877. It cost about £13,000 to build and was designed by Messrs Goldie & Childe of London. An unusual facet of the building was the erection of St Joseph's Schools underneath the church.

In the 1960s the first signs of demolition and slum clearance appeared in the area. Negotiations for the rebuilding of St Joseph's were begun in the early 1970s as the parish entered a long period of decline in numbers of people in the area. A new church was begun in January 1982. The foundation stone was blessed by the Pope at Heaton Park, Manchester in May 1982. The new church was designed by Cassidy & Ashton of Preston, and was officially opened on 30 June 1983 by the Right Reverend Thomas Holland, Bishop of Salford.

St Mary's, Islington (Figure 4)

In 1860 it was decided to establish a third Catholic Mission in Blackburn in addition to St Alban's and St Anne's for those who lived in the 'Nova Scotia' district of the town.

There is a curious legend attached to the formation of this new Mission. It tells how Father Richard Dunderdale came from St Anne's, Manchester to investigate the possibilities of a new Mission in Blackburn. He found what he considered to be a suitable plot of land in Dean Street. However, he could not think of a way to get £500 for building the church. Disheartened, he took the train back to Manchester. During the journey he spoke to a fellow passenger about his need for money to build the proposed new church in Blackburn. The stranger listened sympathetically and the next morning Father Dunderdale received a letter containing a cheque for £500. This Good Samaritan was Mr John Sparrow.

On 13 October 1860, an 'Iron Chapel' was erected in Dean Street. This chapel was dedicated to 'Our Blessed Lady the Mother of God'.

On Whit Sunday 1864 Bishop William Turner laid the foundation stone in Sumner Street of the Gothic Church of St Mary's. The architect was Mr John Cundall of London, and it cost about £5,000 to build. On 4 May 1865 the Church was opened by Bishop Goss of Liverpool. A side altar in honour of St Francis was added in 1887.

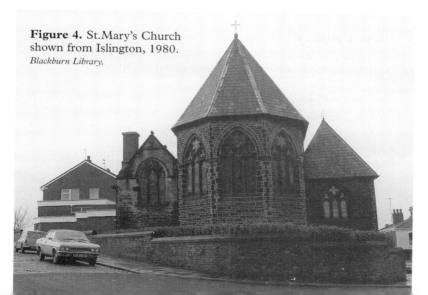

Figure 4. St.Mary's Church shown from Islington, 1980.
Blackburn Library.

St Mary's was situated in an old part of the town and a programme of demolition for most of the houses in the district began around 1968. By the early eighties nearly all the houses that formed the parish were gone. Finally, on 4 November 1987, Bishop Patrick Kelly concelebrated a Mass of Thanksgiving. After a while, the Church was demolished.

St Peter's, Mill Hill

The site which was chosen for St Peter in Chains, Mill Hill, Blackburn was a piece of land off Watson Street on which had stood Eccles Hall. At 4pm on 6 August 1887, the foundation stone for the new school/chapel was laid by Bishop Vaughan, and the Opening Ceremony and High Mass were celebrated by Bishop Vaughan on Thursday 25 July 1889.

The school occupied the ground floor, and the chapel occupied the upper floor, with seating for 750.

A new church was envisaged, and on 18 July 1914 the foundation stone was laid, on a site that was adjacent to the school/chapel, by Bishop Whiteside, the Bishop of Liverpool. However, due to the First World War and a lack of money, it was another forty years before building began. Permission to build a new church was given in 1953, and actual building began on 28 August 1955. The foundation stone was laid by Bishop H V Marshall, and the original stone laid in 1914 was reset. The official opening was 24 June 1956.

St Teresa of the Child Jesus, Intack

The Bishop of Salford, Dr T Henshaw laid the foundation stone on Saturday 29 May 1937 for St Teresa's Church, which was intended to serve the new housing areas in Burnley Road and Intack. The building is on a three acre plot of land between Carluke Street and Bentley Street. It cost approximately £3,000 to build, excluding furnishing. At first it was served from St Joseph's.

Notes and References

1. Smith, Rev Robert, *History of Catholicity in Blackburn and the Neighbourhood*, (nd)
2. Hilton, J A, *Catholic Lancashire: From Reformatiaon to Renewal 1559-1991*, 1994.
3. *Handbook to the Catholic Conference in Blackburn*, 1994
4. Bolton, Charles A, *Salford Diocese and its Catholic Past. Extracts relating to Blackburn*, 1950.
5. Conlon, Mary, *St Alban's, Blackburn 1773-1973*, 1973.
6. Souvenir Handbook of the Sale of Work for Sacred Heart Church, 1935.
7. *Barrett's Directory of Blackburn*, 1942.
8. *St Joseph's, Audley, the Dedication and Consecration*, 1983.
9. Rose, Fred, *Pleasington Priory*, 1986.
10. *St Peter's RC Parish, Mill Hill 100 years*, 1986.
11. *The Blackburn Times*.

Acknowledgements

I would like to thank the staff at Blackburn Reference Library.

13. THE EARLY HISTORY OF CALDERSTONES: AN INSTITUTION FOR MENTAL DEFECTIVES 1904-1959

by Gillian Hall and Susan O'Malley

CALDERSTONES OPENED IN 1922 as a Mental Defective Institution. However, the history of Calderstones goes back much further than this date. A brief examination of this 'pre-history' will illustrate the chameleon-like quality of this large hospital. The history of Calderstones is also a history of wider social changes that occurred throughout the early part of the century. This chapter will begin by looking at why and how Calderstones developed before going on to present a more detailed account of hospital life[1].

In 1898 the Lancashire Asylum Board appointed a committee to report generally upon the question of dealing with 'epileptics and imbeciles', particularly with regard to meeting the 'want' of accommodation in Lancashire's asylums[2]. The Committee concluded that in the light of the 'great accumulation of lunacy cases' the Board should realise its obligation to provide sufficient asylum accommodation. This alleged increase in lunacy was of great concern, not only to Lancashire, but also nationally[3]. There was clearly great alarm surrounding the question of lunacy.

This concern was particularly acute in Lancashire and the Lancashire Asylum Board advocated the building of a sixth asylum and Whalley was chosen as the most appropriate site (Figure 1). However, so great was the opposition to the building of an asylum in Whalley that a public inquiry was held. The inquiry, held in the Assembly Rooms in Whalley, lasted for three days[4]. Of paramount concern at this time was the number of 'insane paupers' (reportedly

Figure 1. Whalley in 1910. *Blackburn Library*

3,136) in Lancashire's workhouses and it was felt that the great
majority of these cases should be confined in 'properly managed'
asylums instead of being left to the punitive regimes of the
workhouses.

Opposition to the building of Calderstones was clearly well
orchestrated. Many local landowners, including such people as The
Duke of Somerset; Colonel Ralph J Aspinall, JP, (Standen Hall,
Clitheroe); HW Worsley Taylor, Esq, KC, MP, Chairman of Quarter
Sessions, Preston (Moreton Hall, Whalley) were represented at the
inquiry by Mr MacMorran KC. Also opposing were the Lancashire
Association of Urban District Councils and the Corporations of
Bury and Bolton. The case for the opposition rested on several key
arguments; for those who owned large estates and property in the
area the issue was one of maintaining their economic value; the
public bodies, on the other hand, were alarmed at the cost to their
ratepayers. All apparently accepted the need for a sixth asylum. In
general the ratepayers of Whalley were in agreement with the
proposed site[5]. The opposition, however, mounted a stringent attack
and pointed to the unsuitability of the land. Expert witnesses were
called to show that the price of the land to be purchased was
excessive. However, it was claimed that savings would be made
because the clay soil was suitable for the manufacture of bricks with
which to build the institution. Another argument put forward in
opposition questioned the exposed position of the site. It was stated
that:

> ...*its exposed position, and its liability to heavy fogs would not be
> conducive to the health of lunatic patients who are particularly liable
> to tubercular complaints*[6].

Mr Worsley Taylor MP was concerned to highlight the high level of
rainfall of the region and the 'coldest, rawest and most penetrating'
air that he had ever known. However, his main concern was that the
town of Whalley would become known for its lunatic asylum rather
than its historical association with the Church and the Abbey:

> *I think you are going to have here, as I understand, an enormous red
> brick building, containing a couple of thousand people and, of course,
> their keepers - I don't know how many they will add up together - in
> the middle of the valley. I venture to think it will disfigure the most
> beautiful valley in this part of the country*[7].

This fact, coupled with the expressed fear that 'bands of unhappy
lunatics' would be exercised along the public highway clearly

distressed the local landowners. In 1906, however, the Home secretary sanctioned the purchase of the Whalley site, subject to the condition that 'no patients shall be exercised on the Mytton Road beyond the point marked' (Meeting of the Whalley Site Committee, 24 May 1906) and the County Architect, Mr Henry Littler, was instructed to submit plans for the asylum.

The final plans were submitted to the Asylum Board in October 1906 and work on the site began in 1907. One of the first tasks undertaken was the laying of the branch railway line and the installation of brick-making machinery. Mr JW Raby was appointed as the manager of the brickworks. As stated earlier, it had been envisaged that the clay soil would be suitable for brickmaking. However, the bricks produced did not come up to standard and Accrington bricks had to be purchased. In July 1910 the contract to build the main part of the institution was awarded to Messrs Robert Neil and Sons, of Manchester. In June 1911 Mr Neil complained that because the bricks were not of a consistent size the cost of laying them was increasing. In fact by November Messrs Neil and Sons were in financial difficulties and had withdrawn their labourers from the site. The contract was then awarded to J Parkinson and Sons Ltd, Blackpool who began work on the site in February 1912.

Just as the building work was about to be completed, the War Office requested that it be used as a Military Hospital and the asylum became Queen Mary's Military Hospital[8]. On receiving the request from the War Office, the Asylums Board agreed to pay a bonus to the building contractors, Messrs Parkinson, for early completion and a revised plan of essential building work was instigated in order to enable the military to take over the hospital as soon as possible. There were on average 420 men employed on the building work. In an attempt to overcome the shortage of labour at this time the rate of pay was increased from sixpence to sevenpence per hour. Over 100 extra 'navvies' were employed to alter the railway line which ran directly into the hospital grounds. With the building work progressing, a Furnishing Sub-Committee was appointed and they set about ordering the necessary equipment and furniture. The records show that 1,000 bedsteads at a cost of 22s 10d each were purchased from A Blain and Sons, Liverpool; 1,000 Caxton chairs at 2s 9d from J Webb and Son, High Wycombe; 100 arm chairs (smokers) at 8s 3d and 148 card tables at 19s from W Higgin Ltd, Bury. Stage equipment was also purchased for the Recreation Hall and a local voluntary group began organising concerts for the wounded soldiers.

Queen Mary's Military Hospital officially opened on April 14 1915 and the first convoy of wounded soldiers arrived on 6 May 1915. Because the hospital had its own railway siding, ambulance trains had a direct link between the channel ports and the hospital. Often trains would arrive at the platform in the hospital grounds carrying hundreds of walking wounded and more serious stretcher cases with the mud of the trenches still on their uniforms. The War Office and the Visiting Committee (appointed by the Asylums Board) had joint responsibility for the hospital during the war. The nursing staff came from the Royal Army Medical Corps along with nurses from Princess Alexandra's Nursing Corps and the Voluntary Aid Detachment. At various times there were shortages of female labour to work in the laundry and local voluntary workers responded by repairing the soldiers' socks. During one week in April 1916, for example, 149 pairs of socks were repaired by volunteers. Some 67,000 British and Allied troops were treated at Queen Mary's during the war and for some time afterwards. Some, unfortunately did not leave. Extra land was purchased to provide a separate military cemetery (Figures 2 and 3) and a suitable approach road. In January 1919 there were still 1,883 patients being treated at the hospital and it was only in June 1920 that the last group of soldiers left.

In July 1920 a newly formed Sub-Committee of Managers, with Mr Travis Clegg as Chairman, appointed Dr Frank A Gill as the Medical Superintendent of Calderstones Certified Institution for Mental Defectives with a salary of £1,200 per annum[9]. Although Calderstones had been purposely built as an asylum for the insane, it now assumed a different role and this was because of the 1913 *Mental Deficiency Act*. Nationally there had been a change of ideas. Lunacy had given way to 'mental defectiveness', which in turn was linked to degeneration and immorality. Mental defectiveness was seen to be inherited. It was also believed that mentally defective people were more fertile and immoral, and, if left to their own devices, would swamp society with incompetence and criminality. The *Mental Deficiency Act* placed a duty upon the Statutory Local Authorities to ascertain the number of mentally defective people in their area and then to provide suitable supervision and accommodation.

The Mental Deficiency Act of 1913 makes provision for dealing with persons who are not sufficiently defective in mental capacity to be technically certified as lunatics, and yet at the same time have not, owing to an underdevelopment of the brain, the capacity for taking care of themselves or of their property, or who may be dangerous to the community by having criminal tendencies. The general scheme of the Act is to place upon the Statutory Local Authorities the responsibility of ascertaining who those persons are in each Authority's Area, and then taking steps to see that they are looked after and maintained either under a system of private guardianship or in Institutions to be provided by the Local Authorities or by voluntary organisations[10].

Calderstones officially opened its doors on 25 July 1921. The number of patients at this time was small. Most of them had come from Brockhall, which was run as an annex to Calderstones until 1933. In fact in the original planning stages it was suggested that a bridge over the River Calder be built to join the two institutions together, however because of the cost, this never materialised. They were all 'working patients' selected because they were capable of helping with the upkeep of the institution. By 1922 the numbers of patients had grown considerably to 1,247 and by 1924 the total number resident at both Brockhall and Calderstones was 2,175. Patients came from other institutions throughout Lancashire. Many were to come and go, however many were to stay for the rest of their lives. Willie Glover died in Calderstones in 1997. He had been a 'resident' since 1924. He was admitted at the age of eight because he was seen to be 'unmanageable'. His mother had given birth to him in Ormskirk Poor Law Institution in March 1915. Under the 1913 *Mental Deficiency Act*, a woman in receipt of poor relief could be certified if she gave birth to an illegitimate baby. As such, Martha Glover was deemed to be a 'moral defective' and she was already in

Figures 2-3. Memorial in military cemetery. *Joe Wharton.*

Brockhall. She died in Calderstones in 1984. These two cases are by no means unique[11].

In overall charge of Calderstones was the Committee of Managers who were a sub-committee of the Lancashire Mental Deficiency Act Committee. The Board of Control, an arm of the Home Office, ensured that local authorities exercised their duties responsibly and that they carried out the due process of law in relation to the *Mental Deficiency Act*. They did this by visiting the institution bi-annually. This resulted in a report which was submitted to the Management Committee. In these reports every aspect of institutional life was commented upon, sometimes critically and sometimes with praise. In terms of the day to day running of the institution, Dr Gill had overall charge and it was his influence that affected the lives of the people who lived there. Directly underneath Dr Gill in the hierarchical staff pyramid was the Matron, Miss Elizabeth Warburton, who like Dr Gill, was responsible for Brockhall staff. Assisting Dr Gill was Dr R B F McKail, appointed as the Senior Assistant Medical Officer. Miss Paterson was the Assistant Matron and Mr McVittie was the Works Foreman. Other staff names only appear in the documentation if they were discussed by the Committee for some reason. The baker, for example cut off two of his fingers whilst operating the bread cutting machine and received £175 in compensation in June 1923. William Edwardson was a former patient at Queen Mary's Military Hospital and he became employed by Calderstones in 1921. He was to work there until his retirement. His wife was also employed there for some time as well as their children[12]. By the end of 1924, the total number of nursing staff was 224.

Calderstones, like most institutions of its kind, was designed to be a self-contained community. Every aspect of life was catered for within its walls. Patients entering were categorised according to age, gender and mental capacity. They were housed in pavilions which were separate from the main administrative buildings. The women's pavilions were on the west side and the men's on the east side. In

Figure 4. Administrative block *Author.*

between was the administrative block (Figure 4) which acted as a 'contraceptive band'[13] for both patients and staff alike. Behind the administrative block was a work block which contained facilities for the shoemakers, the brushmakers, the tailors, the upholsterers and the mat makers. Also nearby was a general bath house, the kitchen, the laundry and general stores. A noticeable feature of Calderstones was the dominant clock tower (Figure 5) and below this a recreation hall with polished wooden floor and stained glass windows portraying the coats of arms of the Guilds involved with the building work. At one end of the hall was the stage which was used for concerts and pantomimes. The pavilions were grouped into seven separate departments, each referred to by number and each having an adjacent exercise area, encased by iron railings. These were known as the Airing Courts. It was in these courts that patients had their daily exercise. It is said that when the railings came down, patients were so used to walking around these court yards in a circular fashion that they continued to do so even though they were 'free' to go further afield. The Medical Superintendent's house was near the main entrance and the houses of other officials were also built in the hospital grounds. Also close to the main entrance was the church (Figure 6) which was used for all denominations and could accommodate up to 740 people. To the north-west of the central 'contraceptive' band there was the machinery and boiler house and also this was where the railway siding entered the main compound from the Hellifield - Whalley line, running past the cemetery and underneath the road. This branch line served not only to deliver wounded soldiers, but also the delivery of coke and coal. The cemetery was, and still is, at the far north east of the main asylum building. It was consecrated on 20 February 1916. In the boiler house there were four Lancashire coal boilers, four steam pumps, and adjoining the boiler house there was the engine, dynamo and accumulator rooms. There was also a large workshop for the blacksmith and a still room in which distilled water was stored. There were two entrances to the institution. At the main entrance there was the gate house where staff collected their keys and a quarter of a mile further along Mytton Road there was a second entrance. Here was where the weigh house was situated. This process of weighing was deemed to be necessary for security purposes. The three storey building of the asylum proper was, as already stated, designed to accommodate 2,000 patients. On each floor there could be approximately 100 patients. This meant that the night dormitories would contain 200 beds.

When the institution first opened, the need for accommodation for staff was acute. Given the long hours of work and the problems of local transport, accommodation was necessary. In 1923 the accommodation for 'subordinate staff' consisted of six detached houses, fifteen cottages, known as Queen Mary's Terrace, six cottages, known as Meadow Cottages and 24 converted army huts. A total of 50 employees and their families occupied these dwellings. Because of a lack of accommodation, particularly for married members of staff, it was agreed that a pair of semi-detached houses for Sub-Officers would be built on land on the north side of the North Entrance facing Mytton Road. A further six Attendants cottages were also built as a continuance of Queen Mary's Terrace on land between Bridge Terrace and the railway line. The building of new and superior houses, however, created a problem. Whilst there was some agreement that the 'best houses' should go to the more senior staff, it was feared that this would cause resentment from staff living in sub-standard 'army huts'. Evidence of staff feeling on this issue materialised in the shape of a petition to the Committee. Because of the problems of staff recruitment, this matter was taken seriously. It is not clear from the records how this problem was resolved. In 1929 a new hostel for female nurses was opened and in 1930 work began on a further eighteen cottages.

Some of this additional building was undertaken by the Institution staff, with some assistance given by the patients. The Chairman's Report of July 1930 states that:

> *Six cottages, part of the scheme for providing permanent brick cottages in substitution for the army huts, temporarily converted into dwelling houses, were nearly completed by the end of the year, and have since been occupied. These cottages were erected by the Institution staff, outside contractors being employed only for tiling and plastering. The interior walls were constructed of concrete blocks made at the*

Figure 5. Calderstones, showing clock tower. *Joe Wharton.*

Figure 6. Church at Calderstones. *Joe Wharton*

Institution, and the cost was £2,318 5s. 5d. or just over £386 per cottage. Two of the huts which became available have been re-erected in the airing courts to provide play huts for juvenile patients.

A block making machine had been purchased in April 1925 and patients worked on this to produce concrete blocks which were used for building Brockhall's initial extension. Several former male patients recalled making these blocks and travelling to Brockhall to build the first male ward which came to be called Ashwood. Patient labour was an important feature of life in Calderstones. Work was compulsory for patients until the *1959 Mental Health Act* and patients often worked for long hours. Farmworkers, for example, would begin their day at 6.30am in the summer months. Patients also worked in the laundry, the kitchen, the stores and the gardens. Their labour also took the form of training, which was viewed as being both therapeutic as well as instilling skills. Many patients worked in the shoemakers, the tailors, the upholsterers, the matmakers, the brushmakers and in the rug room. However, cleaning the wards was by far the major source of employment. One resident recalled his years of working as a ward cleaner and claimed that he was acknowledged as being one of the best cleaners in Calderstones. One year he had even won a prize for the best kept toilets. His prize was in tokens which he could spend in the hospital shop. For this resident, his work was a source of pride and identity.

Indeed several interviewees spoke with fondness about their role as workers. However, this was not always the case. One man still felt angry about his treatment as a cleaner. He recalled that after the second world war the patients had to clean the wards that had been vacated by the military:

> *When the military went they asked for volunteers to go and scrub the wards out. I can remember scrubbing one patch for nearly two and a half hours. I scrubbed away with two hands and asked the charge nurse for more soap. The charge wanted to know why I need more soap. I said so I can get this out of the floor. He said didn't the other staff tell you that's blood - it won't come out*

This same man then went on to describe the 'jumbo', an implement used for cleaning floors and corridors:

> *The corridors needed scrubbing everyday. Jumboing floors every day - a wooden block with lead in the center, brushes on and a long pole. You pushed it up and down after they had put the wax on.*

The jumbo was very heavy and required plenty of effort. For some, however, cleaning the floors of the corridors meant kneeling for hours and one ex-nurse recalled that 'housemaids knee' was common. Another demeaning job, always discussed by those interviewed, was that of collecting the rubbish. This job was often allocated to those perceived as 'trouble' or 'hard'. One man who fell into this category spoke about his work on the 'dubbin cart' which was the vehicle used for collecting the rubbish and, in the early days, the ashes from the fires on the wards.

> *I worked on the dubbin cart - it was a cart on two big wheels and a little wheel at the back to keep it straight and half a dozen running at the side of it. It was like a horse and cart collecting rubbish and taking the stones for the building workers.*

Many patients clearly felt that they should not have been in Calderstones and many attempted to escape and were indeed successful. Staff were always on the alert for this. For example, when patients had to be escorted to the bath house they had to stand on point duty. Similarly, when patients attended the cinema they had to stand at the end of the rows and also switch the lights on every ten minutes. This, of course, was both to ensure that everyone was present, but more importantly, to ensure that male and female patients were behaving themselves. It was a very strict regime. Bed time for some wards was as early as six thirty. This time in particular was remembered by ex-patients as being most undignified. One man recalled that he slept in a dormitory with 112 beds. There was so little floor space that one could walk from one end to the other without touching the floor. Neither was there room for individual wardrobes or lockers:

You could walk from one end to another without touching the floor. Two of you could not get undressed in between the beds. One had to get undressed at the bottom, put a nightshirt on, no slippers in them days, and then carry your clothes, everything that was in, and it was all checked by the night nurse and it was put into another room. Then the night man would come and count them and make sure that all the bundles were there

The collection of clothes was clearly related to security as much as shortage of space and anyone trying to escape had to hide their 'bundles' under their bed.

Recreation was viewed as an important part of institutional life. At least once a week the more able patients were allowed to go dancing. This activity had to be carefully monitored and patients were counted in and out of the wards and the Recreation Hall. Like the cinema visit, the overwhelming concern was to prevent the males and females fraternising with each other. There were strict rules that had to be adhered to by both staff and patients alike:

The males were on one side and the females were on the other and two staff in the center and the patients would have to dance around these two staff. But a sister at one end would note how many dances the girls would have had with one chap or else back to the ward they went. As soon as the music started they all dashed across, picked the girl..and if they hadn't picked the girl within three seconds they would have to go back to the other side - there was no messing about. If they wanted to go to the toilet it was back to the ward and there they stayed.

The punishment for patients not obeying the rules was to deny them their next visit, but for staff it led to a reprimand.

The strict control of the regime affected the lives of staff in many ways. Staff had to get permission to marry and to live outside of the institution. Male staff wore uniform resembling prison officer's clothing which signified their rank. One nurse recalled that:

Discipline was very strict. If you were one minute late you were put on report. Senior staff were always checking on you to make sure you were on time and to make sure your uniform was in condition. If you were on nights you had to use the pegging clock - it was a round clock. When you put your key on the pegging clock it connected to the main office. You had to peg in at ten to the hour and twenty past. This was to keep everyone on their toes and make sure no-one fell asleep.

Staff worked long hours and the pay, although guaranteed through union rights, was not large. They also had to study whilst working a full shift. A retired member of staff, with forty-four years service, recalled his days as a student nurse:

When I started everyone had to go to school. You had two and a half to three years in school as well as on the wards. But students then were supernumary. If you were on duty you went to lectures, but if you were off duty you also went to lectures. The Sub-Officers and the Doctors gave the lectures. I failed my finals twice. There were 34 in my class and only two got through. I went on nights to be able to revise.

Several nurses recalled the Matron's visit to the wards and the fact that the linen had to be arranged with the stripes in linear order and the brass door plates had to be polished daily and 'even the coconut matting was inspected for dust'. As with the patients, male and female nurses were separated by the administrative block and were not supposed to meet whilst on duty. Needless to say this rule did get broken. There was also a night-time curfew and the gates would be locked. Staff had to get permission to stay out later than the specified time. Some nurses, however, where able to climb the gates and frequently did. Many nurses spoke about their work with pride and felt that generally patients were well cared for, especially in terms of their medical well being.

Institutional life for both patients and staff remained static for many years. Significant changes in legislation took place with the passing of the *1959 Mental Health Act*. This in effect meant that patients were technically able to leave the hospital. However, for the vast majority, there was nowhere for them to go. Work was no longer compulsory and more emphasis was put on training and rehabilitation. However, it was not until the implementation of the 1971 White Paper, *Better Services for Mental Health* that real changes were realised within Calderstones[14]. Ward sizes were reduced, becoming more intimate and homely. The railings around the Airing courts were taken down and the 73 Club was opened as a social club for 'residents'. Staff uniforms were discarded leading to a more informal relationship between the carers and the cared for.

It was to be many years before the introduction of community care. In the late 1980s Calderstones was once again amalgamated with Brockhall and, in response to changing government policy, the closure program commenced[15]. There also began a vigorous resettlement programme which led to a large reduction in the numbers of people both living and working in Calderstones'. In 1993 Calderstones became a National Health Trust and the job of resettlement proceeded alongside the development of Calderstones' new role. As in the past, Calderstones, has responded to changing ideas about the treatment of mental health. Calderstones will remain on part of its original site. It will be much smaller and will offer a more specialised service to people who need care and treatment under conditions of medium security. In December 1998 Calderstones closed its long-stay residential part of the hospital. For some patients it had indeed been a long stay.

Notes and References

1. The material used in this chapter is based upon research carried out since the mid 1980s. The authors have studied the official hospital records as well as conducting in-depth interviews with staff and residents. The research project also covered the history of Brockhall and a publication about the history of both these institutions is forthcoming.

2. The committee consisted of Alderman TH Jenkins (Chairman), Dr DN Cassidy (Medical Superintendent of Lancaster Asylum) and Dr J Wigglesworth (Medical Superintendent of Rainhill Asylum). Their Report, Asylums on the Continent, was presented to the Board in August 1900.

3. Dr Wigglesworth gave evidence to the Physical Deterioration Committee of the Privy Council in 1904. Using statistics based upon Lancashire, he claimed that there was an actual increase in the incidence of insanity in the population of the County for the period 1882-1901. It was this evidence that led to the setting up of the Royal Commission on the Care and Control of the Feeble minded (1904-1908).

4. It was stated at the enquiry that the total accommodation provision in the five existing asylums was for 10,825 patients, of which 10,612 were occupied on 13 April 1905, leaving only 213 possible beds.

5. The Parish Council had already shown their approval by consenting to a diversion of a public footpath which ran across the site. Furthermore, a parish election had been fought on the issue with the two candidates who supported the asylum being elected.

6. Whalley Inquiry, p 25, 1905, Lancashire Asylums Board.

7. ibid p 132.

8. The hospital was also used as a Military Hospital during World War Two.

9. Dr Gill, MB, CM, had been appointed as Medical Director of Lancashire Inebriates Reformatory which was opened in 1904. He had been born in Caithness and had graduated from Aberdeen University. Before working in Lancashire, he had worked in Aylesbury State Inebriate Reformatory and had also worked as a Medical Officer in various prisons.

10. Lancashire Asylum Board Annual Report, 26 Feb 1914.

11. The names of these two people are already in the public domain having been featured by television documentaries and magazine articles. Furthermore, through personal contact we know that Mr Glover would have wished his story to be told.

12. The Edwardson family were by no means unique. Several families provided generations of workers. Often they, like the patients, moved between Calderstones and Brockhall.

13. The 'contraceptive band' — so called because it kept the two sexes apart.

14. The White Paper was the result of a number of enquiries (notably the Report of the Official Enquiry at Ely Hospital) which marked a shift in policy towards this group of people. The emphasis of the 1970s was to shift the balance away from institutional care, towards a community-based approach to care.

15. Brockhall closed in 1992. Many residents were resettled and those remaining were transferred to Calderstones.

14. James Hargreaves Morton

by Alan Duckworth

EVERY DEATH IN THE FIRST WORLD WAR was a tragedy; the cutting off of a life before its promise could be realised. It was a story told thousands of times in every town and city throughout Europe and beyond. And yet the story of James Hargreaves Morton seems especially poignant, in part because he was an artist who had not realised all his abilities, but in part because of the faith and belief shown in him by his mother and his sisters. Faith and belief which led them to support him so that he could work as an artist and faith and belief which made them preserve all his work after his death until the last of them died in 1967.

Morton was born on 22 October 1881 at 5 Tockholes Road, Darwen. His father, James Morton, was a cotton cloth looker from Blackburn. His mother Elizabeth, formerly Hargreaves, was from Hoddlesden. He had four sisters; Rachel Ann who was ten when he was born, Sarah who was eight, Fanny who was five, and Alice who was two. There were also two lodgers living in the house. A few weeks after he was born there was a heavy fall of snow which stopped the

Figure 1. Funeral card for James Morton Senior. *Darwen Library*

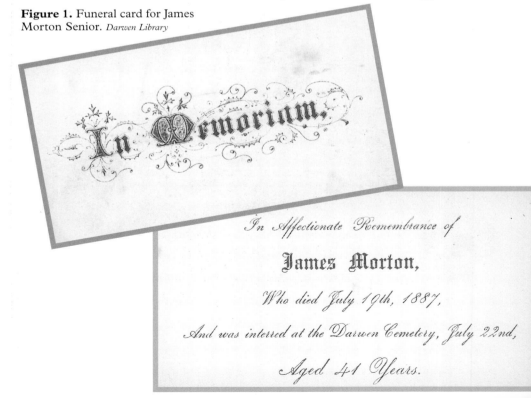

recently introduced steam trams from running. James Morton senior died in 1887 at the age of 41 (Figure 1).

There are echoes here of another moorland family of sisters with a talented brother whom they all doted on. Branwell Brontë also pursued a career as a painter, having a studio in Manningham Lane in Bradford. Unfortunately his talent was not supported by the steadiness and capacity for hard work that Morton had. In the event all the Brontë sisters outshone their brother. Morton's sisters all went to work in the mill, but what undeveloped talent did they have? We can't know the answer to that now, but by supporting their brother, they gave him the chance to give up teaching at the age of twenty-five and devote the next ten years to his art.

Alice was the last sister to die. She was living in Barley Bank Street. The executors were surprised to find the house crammed with Morton's work. There were paintings on the walls, unframed oils, water-colours and pastels in chests, cupboards and drawers all over the house. After being hidden for nearly fifty years, Morton's talent was rediscovered. Exhibitions of his work were held in Darwen and Blackburn.

The light in France is 'different', even in northern France it has a brilliance that you do not get in east Lancashire, but if you study Morton's work you can see that he was interpreting the effect of light just as Cezanne, Renoir, Monet and all the other Impressionists did.

At the time of Morton's birth new ideas about painting were surfacing. Two years earlier Cezanne and Pissarro had first exhibited their work in Paris and earned the label 'Impressionist', offered as an insult by an outraged critic. In 1883 in London the Parisian dealer Paul Durand-Ruel held an exhibition at the Dowdeswell Gallery of works by Degas, Manet, Monet, Pissarro, Renoir and others. It was fiercely attacked by the press. *Punch* in particular exercised its wit in the issue for 5 May 1883 writing that its first 'impression' was that it had entered an exhibition of children's work, and its overall 'impression' that it had wasted the shilling entrance fee.

Despite the combined opposition of uneducated public opinion and the establishment, represented in France by the Salon and in England by the Royal Academy, the Impressionists continued to influence young painters. During Morton's early childhood, Gauguin, Van Gogh and Toulouse Lautrec were producing their best work and by the time he was a pupil at the Higher Grade School, Pablo Picasso, also born in 1881, was embarking on his career.

At the time none of this meant much in Darwen, a town wedded to the industrial arts. There was a respect for the fine arts so long as they showed the high accomplishment and strong narrative content much beloved by the Royal Academy. That this side of Darwen was not generally recognised at the time is indicated by the reaction of a critic who came to see the exhibition held at India Mill in 1868. He wrote in the 16 May issue of the magazine *Freelance* of Darwen as:

> *a kind of absurd little half village, half town with a roughish population, addicted to the various developments of the art of 'puncin' and 'purrin' and given to excesses in morals and beer...and supposing Darwen was not in itself exhibition enough, any such attempt on its part would consist of a display of clog soles, picking staves and flowers of speech.*

However when the writer saw the galleries of oil paintings, water colours and engravings by the likes of Van Dyck, Lely, Gainsborough and Durer, he was forced to abandon his preconception. The truth is Darwen was prosperous enough to promote culture and education, and could provide opportunities for anyone with talent and an appetite for hard work and James Morton had both.

Belgrave British School was where Morton got his early education. The family were living at 4 Willow Street by then. It was opened on 8 November 1879 and quickly prospered. It was an ambitious school and many of its pupils continued full- time education instead of going as half-timers. Mr Jackson of the Manchester School of Art taught freehand landscape, model and geometrical drawing, and every Tuesday and Thursday evening there were drawing classes held by Mr Adams.

In 1893, while in Standard VI, Morton passed an examination in drawing with credit and in the same year was awarded a certificate of merit by the Lancashire and Cheshire Band of Hope Union for an essay on the evils of alcohol (Figure 2).

From Belgrave Morton went to the Higher Grade, or Municipal Technical School, in new premises opened in 1894 at the corner of Knott Street and Union Street. There art was pursued with vigour and exactness, as shown by the subjects examined by the Department of Science and Art : Drawing in Light and Shade; Modelling, Geometrical Drawing; Perspective; Freehand Drawing of Ornament and Model Drawing, all of which Morton passed at both elementary and advanced stages.

Alexander Grubb, head of Blackurn Art School and a well known illustrator, gave lessons at the Higher Grade School. The curriculum also included Chemistry; Magnetism; Electricity; Mathematics;

Figure 2. Certificate from the Band of Hope awarded to James Morton. *Darwen Library*

Physiography; French; English Literature and Woodwork. At the end of the day there was three hours of homework (Figure 3).

The school was opposite the smithy at Shorey Bank and as Annie Proctor writes in her book *The Old School Tie*.

> *The forging of skills and character was carried out day after day to the ringing of the blacksmith's hammer.*

In 1899 Morton justified all that had been hoped of him by winning a scholarship to the Royal College of Art in London. It was provided by G P Holden of Bank Top Mill whose energy and enthusiasm had

Figure 3. Certificate awarded to James Morton for woodwork. *Darwen Library*

done so much to ensure the opening of the Higher Grade School.

Morton moved to London into lodgings at 3 Clifton Gardens off Chiswick High Road, not far from the Hammersmith Bridge, a good spot for watching the Oxford and Cambridge boat race which he did on more then one occasion.

The Royal College was every bit as demanding in terms of hard work and application as anything he had been used to in Darwen, but in what free time he had Morton visited the theatre, attended Bible classes and made excursions into the country such as a typical one to Cobham where he admired the church and almshouses, before resorting to *The Leather Bottle*, a famous inn, for bread and butter and ginger beer.

There was nothing bohemian about his life in London. He was as serious and hardworking as any young man apprenticed to a trade (Figure 4). He took his opportunity however to see the best in contemporary art. In 1899 the International Society of Sculptors, Painters and Gravers was formed with the express intention of promoting Impressionism. Its exhibitions featured paintings by Monet, Degas and Pissarro. We can only guess at his reaction to their work, but we do know that fifteen years later at the Society's 19th London exhibition Morton's own work was shown there.

In 1901 Morton watched the funeral of Queen Victoria at Hyde Park Corner. A few days later he was there again to watch the departure of Kaiser Willhelm II.

Morton succeeded in gaining his associateship of the Royal College. He passed through each of the college's four schools: Architecture; Painting, Modelling and Design. In a letter of reference dated July 1904, his Professor of Painting, Gerald Moira said he had a nice sense of colour and a strong knowledge of drawing, and in another letter dated 4 July 1904 Edward Lanteri, Professor of Modelling, said he had made great progress and had worked extremely hard.

Figure 4. James Morton as a young man. *Darwen Library*

Morton had also had to prove his proficiency in a number of craft skills. He did so ably in stained glasswork, wood-carving (Figure 5), lettering and tapestry. He was now equipped to embark on a career. With no resources of his own, he had to earn a living. Teaching art was the only obvious course open to him.

In 1904 he obtained the post of Assistant Art Master at Darlington Technical School and went to live in the town at 5 Victoria Road. Again Morton became involved in a rigorous timetable of instruction. He taught design, craftwork, and drawing from the antique on two mornings and two afternoons each week. He taught evening classes in freehand, geometrical drawing, and design, and he taught freehand, model and blackboard drawing to pupil-teachers at Northallerton.

He was at Darlington for a year and applied for a number of other teaching posts. The prospect of a lifetime spent teaching must have been losing any appeal it may originally have had. He must have hinted at this on visits home to his family who were now living in Sudell Road. Neither his mother, nor his sisters needed convincing that he had a great talent and would achieve great things given the opportunity to paint full-time. They must have known that neighbours and acquaintances would be horrified to see him give up a good job for what many would see as a frivolous activity, but they made it clear they were willing to support him.

By the end of 1905 Morton had given up his job and was back in Darwen. On 25 August 1905 his mother died.

It was some time before Morton was to see his work regularly exhibited, but his local reputation was growing. His former school, the Municipal Technical School made frequent reference to him in their magazine and used his design on their cover (Figure 6). The *Darwen Literary Society* employed his talent as well (Figure 7). He became a good friend of John Yates, the Blackburn solicitor and water-colourist and the two of them made many painting trips together.

Morton painted many landscapes, in Sunnyhurst Woods and Tockholes, but also on holiday in the Lake District, Cornwall and North Wales (Figures 8-9). He used oils and water-colours, but became particularly skilled in the use of pastels, achieving in that medium effects that could be achieved in no other. He was a keen walker and was associated with the Darwen Naturalists' Club.

Figure 5. Example of Morton's woodcarving. *Darwen Library*

It was in 1911 that he first exhibited at the Walker Art Gallery in Liverpool. Two of his paintings were featured: one of the Liverpool Waterworks at Rocky Brook near Tockholes, the other being a portrait. The Walker Art Gallery did much to promote the careers of Lancashire artists and in the years up to 1916 Morton exhibited there frequently. He also exhibited at Bradford and Hull, and in 1915 achieved the distinction of being featured in the International Society of Sculptors, Painters and Gravers Exhibition alongside the best of contemporary British painting. So completely had the art world been transformed since the turn of the century that this had become a greater achievement than exhibiting at the Royal Academy, which Morton had done in 1916.

To see Morton's work is to be at once impressed with its quality. His friend John Yates, speaking after his death, emphasised the importance of design in his work. Morton admitted this himself writing in undated lecture notes:

Figure 6. Morton's design for the cover of *The Darwen Municipal Secondary School Magazine. Darwen Library*

the decorative aim always ought to be kept in view...a picture is a decorative unit in a scheme of decoration expressed in line and form, pleasantly arranged within certain limits, that is the frame.

Morton believed, as did the Impressionists, in getting outside and painting from nature. He completely vindicated the faith his sisters had shown in him, and with his formidable technical skills, his dedication, distinctive talent, and capacity for hard work, was on the verge of a national, if not international reputation, when war broke out.

In 1914 there had been no shortage of young men eager to volunteer before it was all over, but as the war developed it was clear that technology had changed the way wars were conducted. Cavalry could not be deployed against machine guns and artillery, nor could infantry make much headway without horrific loss of life. The war became static. Trenches ran from Switzerland to the coast of France. Even an advance of a few yards could only be made at an expenditure of lives on a scale never known before. Volunteers were not going to be enough. In May 1916 conscription was introduced. Although he was thirty five, Morton, along with men up to the age of forty-one, was called up. He joined the 66th East Lancs Division.

It was not until January 1918 that Morton, by then a sergeant, went to the front. He arrived in time for Ludendorff's great offensive that all but achieved victory for Germany. Morton was posted to the 2/5th Battalion under Colonel Whitehead. The Battalion was at Hesbecourt in March when the Germans broke through. In the subsequent ten days of fighting the British were forced back over twenty miles almost to Amiens. Paris was threatened and there were fears lest the British Army could not be safely brought home. The 66th Division suffered such losses that it was not possible to reconstitute it and the survivors were used to train American troops who were then arriving in large numbers.

Morton continued to draw and paint while he was in the army and attracted the attention of his Colonel who encouraged him and went to some lengths to obtain materials for him. As the Americans became ready for combat and began to take an active part in the front line, the remnants of the 66th Division were transferred to the 44th Division and Morton found himself in the 1/5th Battalion.

By November 1918 it was clear even to the Kaiser that Germany could not win the war. Revolution threatened at home, mutinies were becoming frequent in the army and navy, and the allies had wiped out all the German advances. Germany was anxious to remain unbeaten in the field and the allies determined to impose severe peace conditions. The fighting continued.

Figure 7. Design for the Literary Society's *Conversazione*. *Darwen Library*

Figure 8. Old houses in Pole Lane. *Darwen Library*

On 6 November 1918 the 1/5th East Lancashires relieved a New Zealand battalion at 3. 30 in the morning near the Mormal Forest. At 6. 30, with 8th Manchesters on their left, they began to advance towards their objective, the road running South from Les 5 Chemins.

German machine guns were in good positions in the orchards and gardens between Petit Bayay and the river Sambre. The fighting was severe and casualties numerous. Morton was among the many who fell.

He lies buried in Row A, grave number 8, in the Communal Cemetery at Pont-sur-Sambre. The brilliant light of northern France shines on his grave.

Figure 9. Coastal scene in North Wales. *Darwen Library*

15. Corporation Park

by Joe Wharton

IN HIS BLACKBURN BASED novel *Avenging Angel* Lorenzo Dali describes Corporation Park thus:

> *I went into the park, a big, boastful enterprise, boarded by villas and fine residences. Its front entrance was almost in the town centre and the furthest of its meandering avenues emerged on a ridge above the town, where there was a fine view of the thousand points of orange light under a sky that was darkening perceptibly like the auditorium of a theatre when the drama is just about to begin.*

The drama began in the early 1850s. Blackburn had received its Charter of Incorporation on 28 August 1851. Before that the town had been run by Improvement Commissioners, and earlier by a body of 12 Police Commissioners appointed in 1803. In 1801 the population was 33,000, by 1851 it had grown to almost 85,000. In that period the town had changed out of all recognition. Formerly it had been an unsightly conglomeration of rickety buildings and narrow streets. These had now been largely swept away. Market Street and Church Street boasted first-rate shops, handsome houses were springing up along Preston New Road, a sewage system had been constructed, a Market Hall had been built, and the new Town Hall with its assembly room, council chamber, police court and cells was admired by everyone.

Blackburn's new mayors went to great lengths to distinguish themselves by promoting public causes. The first mayor, W H Hornby championed the moribund Mechanics' Institute. A later mayor, William Pilkington fought for an infirmary. Before him Thomas Dugdale, mayor from 1854 to 1855, proposed establishing a public park.

Blackburn's rapid growth had left few green spaces where people could escape the urban grime. Many walked up Preston New Road for the exercise and a breath of fresh air, and it was the land bordered by Preston New Road, Revidge and Shear Brow that seemed an ideal site for a park. As can be seen Figure 1 the site contained a wooded valley, reservoirs and a number of quarries.

The land was owned by Joseph Feilden who, agreeing to its

Figure 1. Extract from the 1848 Ordnance Survey, Sheet 62. Six inches to 1 mile. *Blackburn Library*

suitability as a public park, sold 50 acres of it to the Council at the rate of £65 per acre. The Council had to bear the cost of constructing roads on either side of the park, but were able to offset some of this with proceeds from land on the Town's Moor at Nova Scotia, previously sold to the East Lancashire and Blackburn Railway Company. Figure 2 shows the plan of the proposed park.

Work began in February 1855 on the roads at either side of the park. In August 1855 Blackburn contractors Roberts and Walmsley

Figure 2. Plan of proposed park dated 1854. *Blackburn Library*

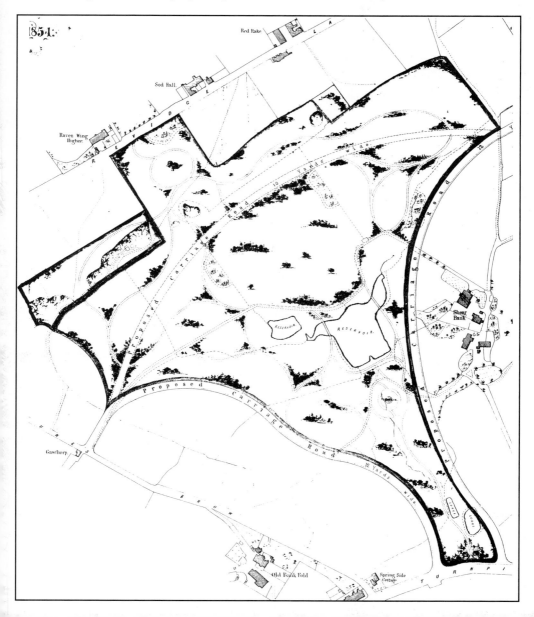

Figure 3. Preston New Road entrance in 1906. *Blackburn Library*

began work on the entrance gateway and the lodge. In October the laying out and planting of the park began under the direction of Mr Henderson, a landscape gardener from Birkenhead. In the following February the perimeter walls were commenced using stone from the quarries in the park. Thomas and John Holden of Blackburn were the contractors for the first class part of the work and William Wright, also of Blackburn, completed the second class portion. In August 1856 work started on the promenades, bowling greens and carriage roads, James Taylor of Burnley being the contractor.

The park was opened on Thursday, 22 October 1857. It was a crisp, frosty morning with brilliant sunshine. The railway companies put on cheap excursions and claimed 14,000 people came to the town by rail. Shops and mills closed at noon. Flags floated from every public building. The church bells were ringing. The police held back the crowds, estimated at 60-75,000, so that there was a space in front of the town hall for the procession to assemble.

At 2pm the Mayor William Pilkington arrived and the procession

could begin. It was led by Mr George Ellis' Band. Next came a detachment of police superintended by Mr Laverty. Halberd bearers came next, and then the Mayor with Alderman Dugdale and Alderman Hoole. The rest of the aldermen followed, along with councillors and invited guests. The clergy came next, then magistrates and pupils of the grammar school led by Mr Thomas Ainsworth, the headmaster. The Rechabites followed with the Darwen Temperence Band, then the United Catholic Brethren followed by Mr Finney's United Brass Band. Another detachment of police with Inspector Holden brought up the rear.

The procession reached the entrance to the park which had been decorated with evergreens and dahlias. Only one of the massive wrought iron gates had so far been hung. The pathways in the park were crowded with spectators. As the procession entered the two cannons on the battery at the top of the park, (trophies from Sebastopol) boomed a welcome. They were manned by men from the Royal Artillery, some of whom wore the Crimean Medal. The roar of the cannons was

Figure 4. Preston New Road entrance, 1906. *Blackburn Library*

Figure 5. The fountain, 1906. *Blackburn Library*

supplemented by the occasional bang as members of the public fired off their own guns.

The procession, half a mile long, threaded its way through the park to the centre point, above the lake and below the bowling greens, where a platform had been erected, from which the park was to be formally declared open.

The Mayor, William Pilkington mounted the platform and the crowd fell silent for his speech. He dwelt on the beauty of the park

Figure 6. The Lake, 1906. *Blackburn Library*

Figure 7. Cannons on the battery. *Blackburn Library*

and the benefits it would bring to all, but particularly to the poorer classes. A balloon was released and the cheer from the crowd drowned his words momentarily. He resumed, referring to the cost of the park and the value of its adornments, expressing the wish that people would respect the park regulations which were shortly to be published. He concluded, saying Blackburn was now on an equal footing with every one of its neighbours in respect of public works. He then declared the park open to the public for ever more.

There was prolonged applause and the cannons roared out again and again. Former mayor Alderman Dugdale was anxious to speak, but it was some time before there was sufficient quiet. He began at last, but his words were interrupted by yet another terrific roar from a cannon. Afterwards a voice from the crowd shouted 'That shut you up!', and there was prolonged laughter.

Echoes of war sounded throughout the day. The Crimean War was not long over and many would have read daily accounts of the battles and hardships faced by the troops in the local newspaper. In that same year, 1857, the Indian Mutiny had broken out with many British soldiers massacred. Blackburn MP James Pilkington, brother of Mayor William, referred to this in his speech at the banquet held later in the town hall's assembly room, blaming the Indian board for mismanaging the situation.

At 6pm the crowds reassembled in the park for the firework display which commenced an hour later with the launch of rockets which released cascades of coloured fire. Some of the set pieces floated on the lake. The principal attractions were the illuminated devices bearing the words 'Town and Trade of Blackburn' and 'The People's Park'. The display was conducted by Mr Bywater of Sheffield.

The people of Blackburn were now free to get to know their park. The splendid archway at the Preston New Road entrance was later embellished by planted trees (Figure 3-4). Three of the four fountains in the park were donated by the Mayor William Pilkington (Figure 5). They were in continuous use until early this century. The large lake (Figure 6) was orignally stocked with ducks and geese donated by local people. Alderman Cunningham donated two black swans. The cannons in the battery at the top of the park survived until the Second World War, though by then they lay on the ground, the wooden carriages having rotted away (Figure 7). A bandstand was built in the park in 1880. This was later demolished and a new one built on the site and opened in 1909 (Figure 8). The war memorial in the garden of remembrance was unveiled on 2 August 1924 by Mrs M J Brown who had lost four sons in the war (Figure 9). The bronze statue by Sir Bertram Mackennal shows the son returning devasted by war to the arms of the motherland.

The statue of Flora, Roman goddess of flowers and spring appeared in the park in 1871. It was the work of Thomas Allen of Liverpool. Legend has it that on certain nights of the year Flora

Figure 8. The new bandstand. *Blackburn Library*

Figure 9. The Garden of Remembrance. *Blackburn Library*

descends from her pedestal and roams the park. In 1951 she was found daubed with red paint and decorated with a sash. A year later she was found lying on the grass with damage to her head and robe. In 1960 she was again daubed with paint and a placard was hanging round her neck. This was all put down to vandalism at the time, but perhaps it was evidence of her nocturnal adventures.

The conservatory was opened on 16 May 1900 and by 1903 the banana plant was bearing fruit. There had originally been a small avairy next to the conservatory. The present one was opened on 5 June 1958 by Mr Walsh, who later donated thirty birds. The broad walk and the paths leading off it to the top of the park were laid in 1863. The work was carried out by unemployed cotton operatives during the cotton famine. In 1944 a spitfire crashed in Blackburn and it is said the pilot parachuted to safety landing on the broad walk.

Lorenzo Dali describes how the park descends almost to the very centre of the town. It has been bringing a breath of the

countryside to factory, shop and office workers for almost 150 years now. Perhaps it is appropriate to end with a description of the park by another writer, Blackburn poet William Billington, who wrote this sonnet on 19 October 1857 to commemorate the opening of the park.

> *Perambulating ' Blackburn's People's Park',*
> *I scaled the rocky ridge of Revidge Hill,*
> *And sat beside the Russian guns to mark*
> *The lakes below that slumbered calm and still;*
> *The white and winding ways, through which a dark*
> *And devious stream of men and maidens strolled'*
> *Before my feet lay, like a map unrolled,*
> *Where land and water formed as fair a scene*
> *As ever slept beneath the soft serene*
> *Autumnal heavens, or blushed beneath the smile*
> *Of rosy Spring, who robes the Earth in green*
> *And golden garb. In this unconquered Isle'*
> *Where Cromwell fought and Milton tuned the lyre'*
> *Such scenes show Freedom's heat still throbs with martial fire!*
> (Figure 10)

Figure 10. The view from the top of the park on opening day. *Blackburn Library*

16. WORKERS' PLAYTIME

by Alan Duckworth

THIS IS HOW THE DAY BEGAN. Allen Clarke, born in Bolton in 1862, began work as a piecer and went on to become a journalist and writer. This is his description of the start of day in a textile town last century. It is taken from his book *Effects of the Factory System*, published in 1899.

> . . .*winter's morning at 5 a.m. Dark and desolate the streets, dark the silent houses and shuttered shops, dark and soundless the huge factories and sombre weaving sheds, dark and forsaken public squares and places, dark the empty schools and solemn churches and stiff chapels, dark now the hotels and beershops, and hushed their tipsy din, dark the tomb-stoned cemetery and withered public park, dark all heaven and earth, save for the far off stars fixed above, and the lonely gas-lamps set at certain distances by man in the dreary world below,- the manufacturing town of Spindleton at 5 o'clock on a cold December morning.*

Just put yourself in the position of the poor mill worker. Imagine! There you are, shivering on a meagre mattress beneath threadbare blankets, supplemented by coats and rag rugs. You're not alone in the bed, but you don't mind that. Even though you've been fighting them all night for a fair share of the covers, you're grateful for their warmth.

If it wasn't so dark, you'd be able to see your breath haunting the bitter air before your very eyes. You could be in a cave of ice, and the snufflings and snorings of your companions could be the sleeping sounds of hibernating bears.

There's another sound! Outside! An oft repeated rattle and garbled cry that grows louder and louder down the street. Suddenly the bedroom window reverberates to a wild tattoo and an ungracious voice enquires if you intend lying there all day.

The bears about you stir and growl, and one, who's been clinging to the edge of the bed all night, rolls out, lumbers over to the window, paws at the frosted glass and snarls a savage reply.

Your early morning call didn't come from British Telecom or your clock radio in those days. It came from the knocker-up. Edwin

Waugh, born in Rochdale in 1817, who became a printer and writer describes the work of the knocker-up in his book *Lancashire Sketches*, published in the 1880's

> *He who has wandered about the city, with observant eye, at dawn of morning, may have seen men,- sometimes a woman,- hurrying along the street, hot-foot, and with 'eyes right', holding aloft long taper wands like fishing rods. These are Knockers-Up, going their hasty rounds, from house to house, to rouse the workman to his labour. They are generally old men, who are still active on foot; or poor widows, who retain sufficient vigour to enable them to stand the work; for it is an employment that demands not only severe punctuality, but great activity,- there is so much ground to cover in so little time. It is like a 'sprint-race',- severe while it lasts, but soon over. And the aim of the Knocker-Up is to get as many customers as possible within as small a circle as possible,- which greatly lessens the labour. A man who has to waken a hundred people, at different houses, between five and six o'clock needs to have them 'well under hand,' as coachmen say. With this view, Knockers-Up sometimes exchange customers with one another, so as to bring their individual work as close together as possible. The rate of pay is from twopence to threepence per week for each person awakened; and the employment is sometimes combined with the keeping of a coffee stall at some street end, where night stragglers and early workmen can get their breakfast of coffee and bread and butter.*

Hours at the mill were from 6 a.m. until 5.30 a.m. with half an hour for breakfast and one hour for lunch six days a week. In the 1840s a Manchester man William Marsden began to campaign for an early finish on Saturdays. The mill owners were aghast, convinced it would be the ruin of them, but his persistence was rewarded and the Manchester workers were the first to benefit from the half day. The Factory Act of 1850 prohibited the employment of women and children after 2 p.m. on Saturdays and gradually this privilege was extended to the men.

Hours for shop workers were even longer: 7.00 in the morning until 11.00 at night six days a week, and 7.00 until noon on Sunday. It wasn't until the 1880s that the employees overcame the resistance of the shop owners and gained an early finish on one day in the week.

There were no holidays with pay until the *Bank Holiday Act* of 1871. The only public holidays were Good Friday and Christmas Day. In Lancashire Christmas Day had never been traditionally a holiday; New Year's Day being preferred.

We assume history is a record of steady improvements and that, as bad as working conditions were last century, they were still an improvement on some unimaginable awfulness in the centuries that had gone before. The evidence suggests otherwise.

In the eighteenth century before the Industrial Revolution had properly got under way, the Bank of England had 47 holidays in the year. All saint's days were holidays, and many workers added 'St Monday' and 'St Tuesday' to the list and hence enjoyed a long weekend. Handloom weavers who were still largely independent, organised their work so that they had at least one day a week off and the day when they took the finished cloth to the 'putter-out' was something of a holiday as well. Samuel Bamford, born in Middleton in 1788, was the son of a handloom weaver. He became a writer and activist on behalf of the workers. In his book Early Days, published in 1849, he describes accompanying his uncle on just such a day. It was called the 'bearing out day'.

> *...my uncle .. would walk deliberately. With a stick in his hand, his green woollen apron twisted round his waist, his clean shirt showing at the open breast of his waistcoat, his brown silk handkerchief wrapped round his neck. A quid of tobacco in his mouth, and a broad and rather slouched hat on his head. So he would appear when setting out on a 'bearing home' journey; whilst I, with my smaller wallet, with my rough jacket, my knee breeches, my strong stockings and shoes, my open collared shirt, and pleasure and glee in my heart and countenance, footed the way as lightsomely as a young colt. Our road then lay up the brow at Alkrington, which was a pleasant footpath through fields . . . and along the highroad to Manchester. It would sometimes happen that warp or weft would not be ready until after dinner, and on such occasions, my uncle having left his wallet in the care of the putter-out, would go down stairs and get paid at the counting- house, and from thence go to the public house where we lunched on bread and cheese, or cold meat and bread, with ale, to which my uncle added his ever-favourite pipe of tobacco.*

The inventions of Hargreaves, Arkwright and Crompton were to banish that way of life for ever. The 'putters-out' began installing the new machinery in their warehouses and handloom weavers could not compete. They had to come and work in these warehouses; the mills, or starve.

As the machinery became faster and more efficient, the mill owners expected the workers to become like machines themselves.

Allan Clarke, again writing on the Effects of the Factory System, describes what it was like.

And all these hours - ten hours a day - spinner and weaver are on their feet: no sitting down; no resting; one must keep up to the machinery though agonised with headache, or troubled by any other complaint. While the engine runs the workers must stand: the machinery cares naught for fatigue, weakness, ailment, sorrow, anxiety for sick husband, wife, or child, at home; grief for a dear one's recent death, maybe the night before; with the motion of the spindles and shuttles no human pain or woe must interfere: the workers must leave all their heart and soul at home when they go to the factory. All they need is 'hands,' and brains sufficient to guide the 'hands' and keep the body out of danger.

There was little relief to be found at home. Houses for factory workers had been thrown up at great speed, with little thought given to the comfort of those who would live there. There is a story that some workers complained to the mill owner, who was also their landlord, that the houses were not fit to live in. 'I didn't build'em for you to live in,' he replied. 'They're just for sleeping in. Mill's for you to live in.'

Angus Reach, a journalist on the *Morning Chronicle*, toured the North in the 1840's. This is his description of the worst slum in Manchester.

The last place we visited is, I am told, the 'worst cellar in all Manchester.' The outer room was like that of others which I had seen, but following a woman who held a light, we proceeded into the inner cellars. They were literally vaults, three of them opening from one to the other. The air was thick with damp and stench. The vaults were mere subterranean holes, utterly without light. The flicker of the candle showed their grimy walls, reeking with foetid damp, which trickled in greasy drops down to the floor. Beds were huddled in every corner; some of them on frames - I cannot call them bedsteads - others on the floor. In one of these a man was lying dressed, and beside him slept a well-grown calf.

Little wonder then, faced with these conditions, that many turned to drink. It was the fastest way out of town. With any sort of home based recreation out of the question, the pub or beershop was the only social institution available to ordinary folk. It provided warmth and light, company, food and entertainment. Many early recreations such as cock fighting, badger baiting, dog fighting and boxing were

Figure 1. Cyclists in Ribchester at the turn of the century. *Blackburn Library*

associated with pubs. The post was delivered to the pub. Newspapers were available there. Many workers were paid their wages in the pub. Alcohol was cheaper than any other beverage available at the time; a pint of beer cost less than a pint of coffee. It had been discovered in 1854 that cholera was spread via polluted drinking water, and milk was often sour and grey with dust by the time it reached the big cities.

With no recreation available in the town and the countryside barred to them by landowners who didn't want gaming rights devalued, the public house was the only resort.

In 1854 there were 126 inns and 186 beershops in Blackburn. By 1860 there were 50,000 beershops throughout the country and offences for drunkenness increased threefold between 1857 and 1876 from 75,000 to 200,000 annually. Little wonder then that the second half of last century saw the growth of the temperance movement and the proliferation of public parks, mechanics' institutions and public libraries in an attempt to offer workers alternatives to the public house.

Attempts to reduce working hours had been going on since 1819 when Robert Peel introduced an act to limit children to twelve hours work a day. In 1847 the ten hour act was passed, but it was not always observed by mill owners. The 1871 Bank Holiday Act created holidays on Boxing Day, Easter Monday, Whit Monday, and on the first Monday in August.

Improvements in transport also had a big impact on the growth of leisure pursuits. The railway had been seen as a means of transporting goods, but it was its ability to move large numbers of people that had most impact. At Whit week in 1848 116,000 passengers left Manchester on cheap excursions, by 1850 that figure had reached 202,000. The railway companies put on special excursions to the races, prize fights, and even public executions. They carried thousands of people to Liverpool in 1849, to watch John Gleeson hang outside Kirkdale gaol.

Another, cheaper, form of transport became available towards the end of the century: the bicycle. In 1878 the Cyclist Touring Club was set up with 142 members, by 1899 it had over 60,000 members. In many ways the bicycle was more liberating than the railway. It brought real independence, a forerunner of the private motor car, but without the devastating impact on the environment. Imagine the open road at the turn of the century, with the only limits on your movement being your own stamina. Here's Allen Clarke again in a more cheerful mood describing a cycling trip to the Ribble Valley with his girlfriend in the book *Moorlands and Memories*.

My lady and I took our bicycles by the train to Blackburn, and at 10.30 in the morning mounted the wheels, and rode along the road to Whalley, on our left Mellor Moor, whence there is a fine view of the Ribble Valley and the river to the sea at Lytham. Our objective was Whitewell and the Trough of Bowland. 'Tis a pretty road from Whalley to Whitewell, through fair lanes and rural land - miles upon miles of land (and yet 'tis said England is overcrowded). It was the fairest of the Autumn time; the time when the heather is purple on the hills and the corn is golden in the vales. The waysides were coloured with red campion, amid the fern and bracken, purple harebells here and there, and the yellow of the hawkbit, and other flowers, as well as the dark red berries of the hawthorn, and the lighter red berries of the dog-rose (which the children call 'itching berries'). A word here about the best way to get to the Trough of Bowland from the Blackburn side. Most cycling guides tell you to start from Clitheroe. Don't! Turn off for Whitewell at Whalley - you thereby save a couple of miles hard climbing, and do not miss any special scenery(Figure 1).

Of course you didn't need a bicycle to get out and about. Victories against landowners, like that of the people of Darwen against the Reverend W A Duckworth, opened up the countryside to walkers. There was a great increase in interest in botany and wildlife. A weaver could pause by the open door of the weaving shed on a hot Summer's day and see the distant hills shimmering in the haze, and know he could be up there for an hour or so after work, enjoying the freedom and the cool evening breeze. Rambling became very popular and local papers devoted columns to the activities of local clubs and gave details of popular walks.

There was recreation for the less strenuous too. There had been a theatre in Blackburn since at least 1787. The Theatre Royal in Ainsworth Street was built in 1816 (Figure 2), and was completely renovated in 1867. It has been said that there was a deep vein of puritanism in Blackburn that caused the theatres to be poorly attended. That may have been true of the middle classes, but when increasing leisure gave the working classes the opportunity, they became enthusiastic theatre-goers. The Palace Theatre in Jubilee Street opened as a music hall in 1899 and had the biggest gallery in Lancashire. Charles Dickens, himself an enthusiastic actor, gives us an idea what it was like on the other side of the curtain in his novel *Nicholas Nickleby*.

And at length the great day arrived. The crier was sent round in the morning, to proclaim the entertainments with sound of bells in all thoroughfares; and extra bills of three feet long by nine inches wide, were dispersed in all directions, flung down all the areas, thrust under all the knockers, and developed in all the shops. They were placarded on all the walls too, though not with complete success, for an illiterate person having undertaken this office during the indisposition of the regular bill-sticker, a part were posted sideways, and the remainder upside down. At half past five, there was a rush of four people to the gallery door; at a quarter before six, there was a least a dozen; at six o'clock the kicks were terrific; and when the eldest Master Crummles opened the door, he was obliged to run behind it for his life. Fifteen shillings were taken by Mrs Grudden in the first ten minutes. Behind the scenes, the same unwonted excitement prevailed. Miss Snevellici was in such a perspiration that the paint would scarcely stay on her face. Mrs Crummles was so nervous that she could hardly remember her part. Miss Bravassa's ringlets came out of curl with the heat and anxiety; even Mr Crummles himself kept peeping through the hole in the curtain, and running back, every now and then, to announce that another man had come into the pit.

It was in the Lyceum Theatre in Market Street Lane that 'animated pictures' came to Blackburn. The first purpose built cinema in the town was the Alexandra in Dock Street, but others soon followed. There have been fifteen cinemas in Blackburn at one time or another, and the local newspapers gave details of what was on offer (Figure 3). Leslie Halliwell was born in Bolton and went on to become a film buyer for television. He describes his first visit to the cinema in his book *Seats in all Parts*.

My mother handed our tickets to a smart young lady in a pillbox hat, but it was not until we had followed her flashing torch halfway up the nearest aisle that I glanced over my shoulder and saw the miracle for myself. The screen was astonishing. It astonished by its size, by its simplicity, and by its gentle brilliance. It was a window through which I could gaze into an incredibly glamorous, magical, monochrome world. And it really did look silver, just as the film magazines said.

Games of football had been played since long before the industrial revolution. They were savage affairs between rival parishes with hundreds of players on each side. Shrove Tuesday was a favourite time for matches and the game would go on until it was too dark to see. People living nearby would board up their windows, knowing if

THEATRE ROYAL, BLACKBURN.

FOR TWO NIGHTS ONLY!!

UNDER   THE

IMMEDIATE   PATRONAGE

OF

HER MOST GRACIOUS MAJESTY AND HIS ROYAL HIGHNESS PRINCE ALBERT.

THE NEW ORLEANS ETHIOPIAN Serenaders!

(FROM AMERICA.)

MESSRS. SANFORD, BURKE, OLE BULL, JUNR., RAINER & SWAINE,

Who have the honour of appearing before

Her most Gracious Majesty, His Royal Highness Prince Albert,

HER MAJESTY THE QUEEN DOWAGER,

Their Royal Highnesses the Duke and Duchess of Cambridge.   Her Royal Highness the Duchess of Gloucester.
Marquis Provenzali and Countess Dietrichstein.   Count A. Patocki the Belgian Minister and Madame Van de Weyer.
The Wurtemberg Minister—Baron Koller.   The Swedish Charge d'Affairs and the Baroness de Cetto.
The French Minister and Countess de Jarnac.

The Duke of Wellington.	The Duke of Somerset.	The Duke of Rutland.	The Duchess of Bedford.
The Duke of Richmond.	The Duke of Sutherland.	The Duke of Cleveland.	The Duchess of Cleveland.
The Duke of Northumberland.	The Duke of Atholl.	The Duchess of Buccleugh.	The Duchess of Buckingham.
The Duke of Grafton.	The Duke of Beaufort.	The Duchess of Inverness.	The Duchess of Grafton.
The Duke of Norfolk.	The Duke of Devonshire.		

The Marquis and Marchioness of Ormonde.   The Earl and Countess of Zetland.
Lord and Lady John Russell.   Sir Robert and Lady Peel.

Will give their **INIMITABLE ENTERTAINMENT**, illustrative of Negro
Life and Character,

On THURSDAY and FRIDAY Evenings,

June 17th. and 18th. 1847,

IN THE THEATRE.

THE FOLLOWING LETTER HAS BEEN RECEIVED FROM THE CELEBRATED VOCALIST HENRY RUSSELL.

GENTLEMEN,   14, Park Place Villas, Maida Hill West, London.
    Although personally opposed to any imitation of the Negro Character, yet from the very great talent evinced in your personification of the Negroes of the United States, and the excellent harmonies of your arrangements of many of the Melodies you sing, it affords me great pleasure in recommending you to the notice of the Musical Public.   I am, Gentlemen, yours truly,

HENRY RUSSELL.

PROGRAMME.

PART I.

OVERTURE	
OPENING GLEE, "De Nigger's Fox Hunt."	FULL BAND.
SONG, "Cynthia Sue."	RAINER.
SONG, "She's black dat's a fact," (*Original*.)	SWAINE.
SONG, "Come, Niggers, arouse."	SANFORD.
GLEE, "Who's dat knocking at de door," (*Original*.)	RAINER.
	COMPANY.

PART II.

OVERTURE	
SONG, "Lucy Neal."	FULL BAND.
SONG, "Who's dat Nigger dare a peeping."	COMPANY.
SOLO, VIOLIN	SANFORD.
SONG, "You'll see us on the Ohio," ...by the American	OLE BULL, Jun.
SONG, "Daniel Tucker, (dat old Song.)"	RAINER.
	COMPANY.

PART III.

SOLO, BANJO, ... by the Prince of Banjo Players,	SWAINE.
SONG, "Ladies here, pretty faces."	SANFORD.
SONG, "Mary Blane."	RAINER.
BURLESQUE ITALIAN OPERA, (*Original*.)	COMPANY.

PART IV.

DUETT, Bones and Violin,	OLE BULL, jun. and SWAINE.
SONG, "Let's be Gay."	RAINER.
SONG, "Buffalo Gals."	SANFORD.

To conclude with the

Celebrated Railroad Overture.

DOORS OPEN AT HALF-PAST SEVEN, TO COMMENCE AT EIGHT O'CLOCK.
BOXES, 2s.; PIT, 1s.; GALLERY, 6d.
Tickets may be had of Mr. WOOD, Bookseller, Old Market Place, where the Box Plan may be seen and places secured.
A change of Programme each evening.

WOOD, PRINTER, OLD MARKET PLACE, BLACKBURN.

Figure 2. 1847 playbill for Blackburn's Theatre Royal. *Blackburn Library*

the ball came through, the players would try to follow it.

By the second half of the nineteenth century football had become organised into something like the spectator sport we know today. Blackburn Rovers Football Club was formed in 1875 and 10,000 people watched them play Darwen in 1880. This match was abandoned when the crowd invaded the pitch. In his novel *The Good Companions* J B Priestly describes the Saturday afternoon ritual.

> *For a shilling the Bruddersford United A.F.C. offered you Conflict and Art; it turned you into a critic, happy in your judgement of fine points, ready in a second to estimate the worth of a well-judged pass, a run down the touch line, a lightning shot, a clearance kick by back or goalkeeper; it turned you into a partisan, holding your breath when the ball came sailing into your own goalmouth, ecstatic when your forwards raced away towards the opposite goal, elated, downcast, bitter, triumphant by turns at the fortunes of your side, watching a ball shape Iliads and Odysseys for you; and what is more, it turned you into a member of a new community, all brothers together for an hour and a half, for not only had you escaped from the clanking machinery of this lesser life, from work, wages, rent, doles, sick pay, insurance cards, nagging wives, ailing children, bad bosses, idle workmen, but you had escaped with most of your mates and your neighbours, with half the town, and there you were, cheering together, thumping one another on the shoulders, swopping judgements like lords of the earth, having pushed your way through a turnstile into another and altogether more splendid kind of life, hurtling with Conflict and yet passionate and beautiful in its Art. Moreover it offered you more than a shilling's worth of material for talk during the rest of the week. A man who had missed the last home match of 't'United' had to enter social life on tiptoe in Bruddersford.*

There was a section of the community however for whom no organised recreation was necessary: children. All they needed was a strip of pavement under a gas lamp. Skipping games, singing games, hop-scotch, whip and top, marbles; these were the recreations of children before television, computers and videos. Early planners made little provision for adult recreation when they built the streets of terraced houses, and none at all for children, but the roof of an outside toilet could be the deck of a pirate ship, and any scrap of waste land the jungle, or a desert island.

In the early nineteenth century when children were working twelve hours a day, opponents of moves to reduce their hours pointed out that children could be observed playing out after their work was

Figure 3. Cinema attractions, 5 August 1938. *Blackburn Library*

finished, so clearly they were not exhausted. How it must have galled them to see energy they might have got a profit out of being wasted in play! Fortunately enlightened opinion prevailed, hours were reduced and the 1833 Factory Act introduced the half-time system, ensuring that children spent at least part of the day at school.

The 1870 Education Act made elementary education compulsory and the consequent improvement in literacy opened up new opportunities for recreation. Comics such as *Magnet, Gem, Chips,* and *Comic Cuts* began to flourish, and public libraries opened up the world of books to any child with clean hands and nerve enough to approach the librarian. Robert Roberts in his book *The Classic Slum,* describes a child's first foray through the august portals.

Joining the library sixty years back was, for a child, an essay in adventure. Snuffy went, nerves tensed, cap in hand, down the long, dark ramp, eased himself through the swing doors and tiptoed to the counter. Beyond on a stool, bathed like a priest in holy calm, sat Mr Shadlock himself, deep in the racing handicap book. The boy stood for a time in respectful silence, then he sighed, sniffed, shuffled twice,

Figure 4. Morecambe promenade in the Edwardian era. *Author*

coughed politely through his hot fingers, and at last, his heart pounding, he dared to put the question. 'P-please, sir, could I'ave a joinin' form, sir?' Mr Shadlock pursued his studies. The minutes trod softly by. A gas jet belched delicately behind its frosted globe. The wall-clock tittered. Snuffy drew breath and tried again, but the words stuck in his gullet; a thin, foolish bleat threaded the silence. He blushed scarlet, licked his dried lips and turned to go. Then Mr Shadlock spoke, suddenly, violently. 'Eh?' Panic-stricken, the boy stuttered into

speech. 'Please, sir, could I - could -' Like a bomb the Librarian burst among the faltering syllables. 'Out of it!' he roared.

Finally we come to the annual holidays, the main leisure event of the year for young and old alike. At one time the best the poor could hope for in the way of a change of scene was to go fruit picking, or stay with friends in the country, but gradually, especially in Lancashire, the custom of taking a few days holiday during the local festival, or wakes, became common. People would go on excursions to the Lakes, or Derbyshire, but the seaside was the favourite resort. Holidays with pay were unheard of for ordinary people, but holiday clubs were set up so people could save for them.

The resorts of the Lancashire coast attracted thousands. The benefits of sea-bathing had been extolled since the early eighteenth century. It was claimed sea-water could cure everything from cancer to corns. The royal family had set the fashion, visiting Brighton and building a pavilion there. Soon quiet seaside villages like Southport, Lytham and Fleetwood were becoming popular resorts.

Blackpool boomed during the second half of the nineteenth century. The North Pier was built in 1863, the new promenade was opened in 1870 and the 500 feet high Blackpool Tower was opened on Whit Monday 1894. The illuminations began in 1912 when decorative lights were set up to celebrate the opening of a new stretch of promenade near the Metropole Hotel.

Morecambe developed more slowly than Blackpool, but the arrival of the railway made it more accessible and the resort became particularly popular with Yorkshire people. Some even bought houses there and commuted to work in Bradford or Leeds every day (Figure 4).

Before the last war most people just had one week off in Summer. They would book accommodation in their favourite boarding house well in advance. Usually they provided their own food. The landlady would cook it and charge one shilling a week for the use of the cruet.

It is said when Charlotte Brontë first saw the sea, she was so overcome with emotion, she burst into tears. We can be fairly certain the Darwen tripe dresser, struggling along the platform of Darwen station with his family and a heavy trunk, wasn't so sensitive.

'What have you got in the trunk, Bill?' the porter asked him.

'Tripe,' Bill replied, 'enough for seven of us for t'week.'

CONTRIBUTORS

1. GHOSTIES AND GHOULIES AND LONG-LEGGETY BEASTIES
11. DARWEN TOWER
15. JAMES HARGREAVES MORTON
16. WORKERS' PLAYTIME

Alan Duckworth was born in Halifax, brought up and educated in Bradford and Leeds, and crossed the border into Lancashire in 1971 on taking up a post at Blackburn Library. He has since worked at Whalley, Chorley, Accrington and Lancaster libraries and is now Local Studies Assistant for the new Blackburn Borough, dividing his time between Darwen and Blackburn libraries. He has published short stories and articles in *Yorkshire Life* and *Lancashire Life*, as well as a number of books notably *Darwen;s Day* and *Light on Old Lancaster*.

2. THE HARTLEYS: TWO HUNDRED AND SIXTY-ONE YEARS IN THE TEXTILE INDUSTRY

Hubert Hartley was born in Blackburn in 1922, the second of four sons. He began school at three and left at fourteen to become an apprentice fitter at the British Northrop Loom Company. At eighteen he joined the Navy and served in the Fleet Air Arm. He married in 1948 and worked in various mills in the locality, being made redundant three times as mills closed down. Having spent many years at night school to obtain textile qualifications, he recently returned to complete a computer course. In 1970 he was appointed a JP.

3. Canal Boat Building in Blackburn

Mike Clarke has been researching the Leeds & Liverpool Canal for thirty years. Over a five year period he restored and lived on one of the last wooden motor boats on the canal and has written its definitive history, *The Leeds & Liverpool Canal, a history and guide,* which was published in 1990. For many years he was employed on restoring a wide range of industrial machinery, from steam engines to textile machinery, from water mills to wooden boats. Today he is a self-employed industrial historian with an international reputation. His current major research project is a history of European waterways.

4. The Borough of Darwen Spitfire

Graham Groom was born in Bolton in 1964 but has lived in Darwen from the age of five. He has worked at Darwen Library since leaving school and gained a BA(Hons) degree in Library and Information Studies as a mature student from Manchester Polytechnic. He is the author of a number of books on Darwen, including the best selling *Aesque Labore Nihil: Historical and Contemporary Jottings on Darwen, 1889-1993* and has written for the *Darwen Advertiser and News* and *Red Rose Magazine.* In 1998 he self-published *The Carry On Encyclopedia: An A-Z of Carry On Characters* which sold out within three months of publication.

5. THE LION OF NORTH LANCASHIRE WILLIAM BEESLEY, CHARTIST

William (Bill) Turner was born in Haslingden in 1931. He is married with one daughter. He left Haslingden Modern School in 1945. Thirty-six years later he gained an Honours degree with the Open University. After a variety of labouring jobs and two years in the army, Bill worked in the electricity supply industry up to his retirement as Principle Assistant in Management Services. He has been a Justice of the Peace since 1968. He has long been interested in local history. His publications include three books on the *Accrington Pals* and a book on the handloom weavers' riots in East Lancashire in 1826, entitled *Riot!*

6. BLACKBURN AT THE POLLS

Matthew Cole was educated at St Silas' Junior School and Queen Elizabeth's Grammar School, Blackburn, and has taken an active interest in the town's history for two decades. He is now Head of History at Cadbury Sixth Form College in Birmingham, and lectures for the Open University. He has written and broadcast regularly on history and politics, contributing to, amongst others, *Modern History Review,* the *Lancashire Evening Telegraph,* and the output of BBC Radio Lancashire. He is the author of *Blackburn's West End* (1994) and *Blackburn's Shops at the Turn of the Century* (1996), both by Landy Publishing.

7. The Blue Plaque Trail of Darwen

Mary Whittaker has lived all her life in Darwen. She is married to Henry and they have two grown up sons. She was educated at Holy Trinity School, Avondale Secondary School and Blackburn College. Mary's interests include photography, knitting, embroidery, local history and reading. She is a member of the Friends of the Chalet School, and has contributed to their Annual. Mary is also a member of the Daniel O'Donnel Fan Club.

Jan Gill was born in Manchester, although she grew up in Macclesfield. She moved to Darwen in 1992. She was educated at Macclesfield, Manchester and Bolton, and graduated from Bolton Institute of Higher Education with an Honours Degree in Philosophy and Literature. Jan's interest include photography, history, reading and embroidery.

8. Charles Tiplady

Jim Heyes was born in Blackburn in 1947 and grew up in the Bank Top area of the town. He was educated at Queen Elizabeth's Grammar School, Blackburn until 1964. Starting work at Blackburn Public Library, he became a qualified librarian and is a Fellow of the Library Association. His interest in local history was inspired by the lively weekly articles on the subject in the *Blackburn Times* by George C Miller. Jim has written a number of periodical articles and other material on local history, principally about the Chorley area, where he was formerly employed and now lives.

9. OUT ON LOAN: POPULAR READING IN BLACKBURN AND DARWEN

Robert Snape has a long standing interest in the provision of popular reading through public libraries. He completed a doctoral thesis in this subject in 1992, which was later published as a book *Leisure and the Rise of the Public Library*. He has lived in Lancashire all his life and has worked in Blackburn and Preston public libraries at various stages in his career. He is currently employed as Head of Learning Services at Myerscough College. He lives in Ribchester and is married with two children.

10. EXPERIENCES OF AN IMMIGRANT IN BLACKBURN

Ashok Chudasama was born in Dar Es Salaam in 1946. His family originated in India. He came to Blackburn in 1964 to work in the textile and electronics industries, before obtaining a BA Honours degree in Applied Social Sciences at Preston Polytechnic. He has since worked for Blackburn Council in the Housing Department, the Personnel Department and the Economic Development Department. He is currently Industry and Education Liaison Officer in the Education and Training Department.

12. A History of the Roman Catholic Church in Blackburn

Stephen Martin Child is Blackburn born and bred. He attended Queen Elizabeth's Grammar School, Blackburn. On leaving he started work at Blackburn Library. He studied at Loughborough School of Librarianship for two years and became a qualified librarian. He was Reference Librarian at Blackburn for several years. He has been Deputy Librarian at Burnley Divisional Libraries for the last twenty two years, before taking early retirement. He is the Secretary of the Burnley Historical Society, the Archivist for Pleasington Priory and graveyard, and Treasurer for Pleasington Priory CAFOD (Catholic Fund for Overseas Development). He is currently researching the history of Pleasington. He is also a voluntary warden for the Woodland Trust and a fanatical supporter of Blackburn Rovers. His other interests are hiking, cycling and his dog.

13. The Early History of Calderstones: An Institution for Mental Defectives

Gillian Hall has lived for most of her life in the West Lancashire village of Banks. In 1981 she became a full-time student and graduated from Edge Hill College, Ormskirk with a degree in Community and Race Relations. She then completed an MA in Crime, Deviance and Social Policy and it was during this time that she met and began working with her co-author Susan O'Malley. With some initial funding from Edge Hill College, she began to collect oral histories from residents and staff at Calderstones

Hospital. Gillian and Susan's research has since developed to cover the history of Brockhall Hospital along with that of Calderstones. They have produced several papers in relation to their research and they are currently writing a book which covers the history of both hospitals. Gillian is a full-time lecturer in Sociology at Liverpool John Moores University and a part-time wife, mother and grandmother. Susan O'Malley works in Bolton as a Social Worker. She lives in Liverpool with her partner and three year-old daughter.

15. CORPORATION PARK

Joe Wharton was born in Oldham. When he was a child his father took a farm in that part of Yorkshire north of Clitheroe that is now Lancashire. Joe grew up working on the farm. Later he worked as a grave digger, a dry stone waller, and a nurse. He has completed the London Marathon on a number of occasions and is an adventurous walker, having walked the fearsome 4 Peaks Walk: Ingleborough, Whernside, Pen-y-ghent and Pendle Hill. He has already written an account of that adventure and takes up his pen again in pursuit of his other great interest: local history. He knows the Blackburn area well, having worked in its hospitals. Joe is married to Linda and they have 2 children Nathan and Ellie.

INDEX OF PLACES

INDEX OF PEOPLE